THE SYMBOLS SPEAK

An Exposition of the Revelation

By

Dr. Lillie S. McCutcheon
Columbus, Ohio

D1562561

Reformation Publishers
Steven Williams, Editor
P. O. Box 618
(800) 765-2464

The Symbols Speak (Revised)
By Lillie S. McCutcheon

First published in 1964 as *The Symbols Speak*

It is estimated that more than three thousand religious belief systems exist in the United States. Many of God's children are deceived, divided and scattered. This book is not written to condemn any Christians, but to expose the systems of religion that divide them.

"Make every effort to keep the unity of the Spirit through the bond of peace. There is one body and one Spirit just as you were called to one hope when you were called—one Lord, one faith, one baptism; one God and Father of all, who is over all and through all and in all" (Ephesians 4:3-6 NIV).

Scripture quotations marked (NIV) are taken from the HOLY BIBLE, NEW INTERNATIONAL VERSION. NIV. Copyright © 1973, 1978, 1984 by International Bible Society. Used by permission of Zondervan Publishing House. All rights reserved. All others are from the King James Version.

Printed in the United States of America

First Printing, 3000 copies March, 1999

Reformation Publishers, PO Box 618, Jackson, KY 41339-0618
1-800-765-2464
Fax 1-606-666-9990
RPublisher@aol.com

Steven V. Williams, Publisher

To the Church of God wherein my soul found new
birth, spiritual nurture, inspiring vision, and
eternal faith, this book is dedicated, by
one of her devoted daughters.

Acknowledgments

Grateful appreciation is expressed to James and Maxine Sanders for their diligent proofreading and typing of the manuscript. The book would not have been completed without their faithful efforts and skillful use of computer technology. Their enthusiastic and prayerful support encouraged me from the beginning to the completion of this project.

Preface

Will Jesus come to establish a materialistic kingdom in Jerusalem? Is there really an anti-Christ? Do we believe in a battle at Armageddon? Is there actually just one church? Are there two resurrections? Is hell a real place? What is heaven like? These questions demand scriptural answers. It is imperative that we should not only know these answers for ourselves, but also endeavor to carry the candle of prophecy to illuminate the pathway of fellow travelers on the road toward eternity.

The church is not left without a light of prophecy. The Spirit and the Word offer more illumination to us than the cloud and pillar of fire provided for ancient Israel. Our dilemma is not an eclipse of light; rather it is that our spiritual eyes fail to comprehend prophetic vision. By the medium of intriguing symbols found in the Revelation, the author of *The Symbols Speak* endeavors to vividly portray the position, purpose, and power of the New Testament church in all ages, giving chief emphasis to the church of today.

This book is not a commentary on the Revelation. Rather it is a brief exposition, in simple terms, prepared for the common layman. It is desired that the reader will make a more comprehensive study of the book of Revelation after reading this limited introduction.

The reader is urged to read from the Bible the entire Scripture passages noted at the chapter headings and subtitles in this book. The enclosed picture chart will also prove helpful as you study the parallel themes presented in their chronological order.

It is the author's prayer that your life may be enriched, and that the church may be awakened to her responsibilities and resources for reformation in "today's world."

Contents

Introduction

Periodically God places a true visionary within the church, one to whom He entrusts divine insight and revelation of Biblical truth. Such vision is not one of more people, multiple programs and plans for buildings, but a vision of those eternal values that will stand the test of time.

Dr. Lillie S. McCutcheon was such a divinely gifted visionary. Humble and obedient, in scriptural study, she sought after the deep things of God. Her desire was to know Christ and serve the church for which He died.

It was through this persistent passion for truth that the scriptures came open to her. To hear her preach, teach, or present the lectures on Revelation, one was soon convinced of her visionary giftedness. More than reading into the text (eisegesis) what some want it to say, Sister Lillie was able to see clearly what God was saying to the young church through the use of the symbols. Typology and numerology became fertile fields for unforgettable sermons that continue to speak though her voice is silent.

The church of the 21st century needs the clear teaching of Lillie McCutcheon, especially as it pertains to the New Testament book of Revelation. Confronted by the "contrary winds of doctrine" (Eph. 4:14) from pulpits and much fictional literature, we have more confusion than clarity. Because of this theological confusion, many are seeking for a sound, rational, Biblical approach to this ancient text.

While recognizing that the overarching theme of the book of Revelation is one of ultimate victory and triumph for the Christian Church, she does not ignore our desire to understand the symbols contained therein. With homiletical skill and visionary insight she shares with us the meaning of the book for today and tomorrow.

This revised edition is commended to the total church. Persons of all faiths seeking to understand the scriptural teachings regarding last things will especially benefit from reading this book. It should be included in every pastor's library, be available to all church school teachers, and in the homes of all church families.

John was in the "Spirit" on the Lord's day (Rev. 1:10). May you sense God's Spirit revealing truth to you as you study the Bible with Dr. McCutcheon.

Arlo F. Newell
May 1999

Dr. Arlo F. Newell served as Chairman of the General Assembly of the Church of God Anderson, Indiana for seven years. Having served as pastor for twenty-five years, he completed his ministry as Editor in Chief of Warner Press, publishing house of the Church of God, retiring in June of 1993. He currently serves the church as an evangelist and Dean of Springfield Pastors' School.

The Symbols Speak

CHAPTER I

THE LAST BOOK

"Earth recedes; heaven opens before me," exclaimed the Christian whose last chapter of life neared completion. The first impulse of loved ones near the bedside was to arouse the dying man from what appeared to be a dream. But the faithful saint whispered, "It is not a dream; it is real; it is beautiful!"

A solemn stillness fell upon the room. The final paragraph of the famous evangelist's life had now come to the last sentence. William placed his ear to the lips of his dying father, listening intently to hear his words. Death's silence was broken as a feeble tongue uttered, "God is calling me, and I must go." His uneven, terminating breath placed a period completing the ultimate phrase inscribed in his life's story. An unseen angel closed the life book of D. L. Moody, bound it with the black binding of death, and placed it gently in heaven's library. To those who loved him, the last words of D. L. Moody became immortal.

God has spoken some last words too—words omnipotent, omniscient, and pregnant with life rather than death. No words that fall from mortal tongue could ever compare with the utterances of the Spirit so divine. The magnificent chapters of the Revelation disclose God's final words to humanity. The Apocalypse climaxes the glorious revelation of Jesus Christ and the great redemption story woven throughout all the sixty-six books of Holy Scripture. God spoke through the pens of approximately forty different authors, over a period of more than a millennium and a half. Some authors were highly educated; others were fishermen, herdsmen, or tax gatherers. Various forms of writing have been included: historical, narrative, codes of law, proverbs, hymns, drama, biography, odes, epistles, and prophecies. All these reach a zenith of splendor in the transcending glory of the Alpha and Omega of the Apocalypse. No preacher has heralded his greatest message until he has echoed again the trumpets of the Revelation. No eyes have seen truth for today and prophecies for tomorrow more vividly expressed than those who behold the last paragraphs of God. "Blessed is he that readeth, and they that hear the words of this prophecy, and keep those things which are written therein: for the time is at hand" (Rev. 1:3).

Last things often hold strange and mysterious significance. God's last revelation to man reveals the Christ who is "the first and the last." We hear Him speak of the last day, last trumpet and the last judgment. We bend our ear to the voice of God as He utters final prophecies to His children; and to all that love Him, His words are immortal. Every reader is compelled to cry, "Earth recedes; heaven opens before me!"

Strange as it may seem, there are some individuals who will not regard the Revelation as prophecy. They believe it was only a veiled way of communication, used by early Christians to bring comfort to one another, and at the same time protect themselves from the wrath of reigning Roman emperors. Others believe it is prophecy to be fulfilled after the Second Coming of Christ. They maintain that the clock of prophecy stopped at Calvary and will not "tick" again until our Lord's return. But a careful study reveals that it is the prophecy of the church, beginning with Christ's first advent, depicting its conflicts with sin and Satan through all ages, then climaxing with the Second Coming of Christ.

The Revelator introduces the prophecies expressing that God's purpose is "to shew unto his servants things which must shortly come to pass" (Rev. 1:1). The initial point for these prophecies is obviously marked by Christ's first coming as the author relates, "Jesus Christ who is the faithful witness, and first begotten of the dead, and the prince of the kings of the earth. Unto him that loved us, and washed us from our sins in his own blood . . ." (Rev. 1:5). All this transpired at our Lord's first coming when He paid the price of redemption and established His church. The prophecies, which were shortly to come to pass, began their fulfillment in the first century and continue through all ages of time. When the Lion of the tribe of Judah has opened the last seal; when the seventh angel has sounded the final trumpet; when the last great battle has been fought; when Babylon has fallen Satan is defeated—then comes the great climax of Christ's second coming! John describes the scene shouting, "Behold, he cometh with clouds; and every eye shall see him, and they also which pierced him: and all kindreds of the earth shall wail because of him. Even so, Amen" (Rev. 1:7).

What could be of greater interest to the Christian than to study the prophecies, which lie between Christ's first and second advent? Which ones have been fulfilled? What is yet to come? As eagerly as the ancient Jews searched the Old Testament writings for prophecies of the Messiah's first coming, we, the Christians of today, search for New Testament prophecies of His return.

The Title

Every author is aware of the necessity for choosing an interesting title for his writings. How wisely John chose the inscription, "The Revelation of Jesus Christ" (Rev. 1:1). In the Fourth Gospel, John refers to the Lord as the Son of God, the divine Teacher, the Bread of Life, the great Intercessor, and the crucified and resurrected Christ. He depicts many other portraits of the humble Galilean, but nowhere in the Bible is He revealed in such glory and majesty as in the Revelation. Here He is magnified as "King of Kings," "Lord of Lords," "Eternal Victor," "Alpha and Omega," and the "Glorified Christ." How incomplete the Scriptures would be if they were bereft of these portraits!

The Author

God Himself is the Author of these last paragraphs in Holy Writ, even as "all scripture is given by inspiration of God" (Rev. 1:1; 2 Tim. 3:16). John was chosen of God to be a pen in the Master's hand. Indeed, who would be better qualified to reveal the Christ? John, the beloved disciple, he who leaned upon Jesus' bosom, was the most intimate, earthly friend of our Lord. This faithful disciple had already served as God's scribe to pen the Fourth Gospel and three epistles that bear his name.

John had heard Christ say, "I am the way, the truth, and the life." He heard Him cry, "Follow me," "Thy sins be forgiven thee," and many other sayings revealing Christ as God incarnate. His presence at the Transfiguration prepared him to behold even more glorious splendor. Years had now past since he last saw Christ as He departed through the clouds at Mt. Olivet. Imagine the thrill in the soul of the sainted apostle when this same Jesus appeared to John on the Isle of Patmos! He was no longer in the seamless garment of the poor, but clothed in the rich vestments of heaven. Searching for words to describe the Christ, John penned, ". . . the Son of man, clothed with a garment down to the foot, and girt about the paps with a golden girdle. His head and his hairs were white like wool, as white as snow; and his eyes were as a flame of fire; and his feet like unto fine brass, as if they burned in a furnace; and his voice as the sound of many waters" (Rev. 1:13). No wonder John fell at the feet of Christ in fear as he beheld Him whose "countenance was as the sun shineth in his strength"(Rev. 1:16). It was not a dream! The Master spoke! His words were the familiar entreaty, "Fear not." How often John's soul had been strengthened by those two words. Christ assured John that He was the same Lord who was dead but is alive forevermore, and has the keys of hell and of death (Rev. 1:18). John was commissioned to write the things he had seen, things, which are, and the things which shall be hereafter.

 John participated in divine worship—the highest act humanity is privileged to experience. True worship opens the sanctuary of the soul, and the infinite God communes with finite men. The eyes of the soul become as sanctuary lamps aglow with the glory of Christ's majesty. Pure hearts where Holy Spirit fire is aflame and prayer ascends as incense. The human intellect becomes a chancel where God performs a divine miracle and the will of man is surrendered unto his Lord. Mortal lips are made a pulpit to proclaim an immortal faith. The tongue becomes an organ to render perfect praise. Let our prayer ever be "Lord, teach us to worship in the Spirit that we too may see the Christ."

When and Where the Book Was Written

At the time of the writing of the Revelation, sixty-three years had passed since Jesus had been crucified. These were years of persecution, trial and death for many of the followers of the Christ. A great portion of the first century had become a trail of human blood. Of all the apostles, John alone was exempt from the death of a martyr. In the year A.D. 95-96, the tyrant, Domitian, banished John to the lonely Isle of Patmos, sentencing him to hard labor in the lead quarries there. Patmos is sometimes called the "brown gem" of the Aegean Sea—not because of its beauty, but because of the great events which transpired there. This island is some sixty miles off the coast of Asia Minor. It is barren and desolate, only ten miles long, and narrows in the middle to almost an isthmus. A range of mountains rising to the height of eight hundred feet provides a grand stage for the visions of John. Visiting Patmos today, you would find the eleven-hundred-year-old monastery of St. John erected on top of these mountains. The trumpets, which sounded there, still echo in the Scriptures.

According to historical records, John was recalled from exile when Domitian was silenced by death, and the humane Nerva ascended the throne as emperor. The aged apostle, too feeble to continue public ministry, often pastored in the humble quarters of his home. John died and was buried at Ephesus after completing a life of approximately one hundred years.

Language and Purpose

While it was no doubt written with letters of the Greek alphabet, the Revelation is an amazing combination of symbols and word pictures. This is a language based on analogy. For example, a lion is a symbol of courage; a lamb, a symbol of meekness; a bear depicts cruel, bloodthirsty characteristics. The book also includes sacred objects, such as golden candlesticks, altars, etc. To symbolize great spiritual truths, Jesus many times used this manner of conveying thought in his parables. He spoke of "the vine and branches." He referred to Herod as a "fox." He compared the righteous to sheep and the ungodly to goats.

The interpretation of words can become very confusing. The same word may be used in a number of ways with varied renderings. However, symbols do not change in meaning. The lion delineates courage and power in the twentieth century as much as it did hundreds of years before Christ when Daniel used prophecy.

Another reason for the veiled language of symbols was to assure safety for the early Christians. No man could be charged in court because he had written or read symbolic literature. Understood by the Christian, its meaning was hidden from the enemy; thus, these writings were preserved.

In this manner God fulfills His purpose for the book. In ages of despair it gave courage and hope of eternal victory to millions suffering persecution and death. Today it is our lamp in a sin-darkened world. It warns the reader of dangerous periods in the destiny of the church. The truth in its pages challenges the church of today to engage in the final conflict of the ages. Here the Christian will find a new edge for his sword of the Spirit. Faith becomes strong in the promise of final victory. Love will overcome hate. Light will put out the darkness. Good will overcome evil. Truth will destroy error. Satan will be defeated and Christ, the Conqueror shall forever reign. This the prophecies proclaim!

John Dedicates the Book

The ministry of John was shared by many congregations. He had especially nurtured seven churches in Asia Minor. He lists them in the same order he would have visited them on the main road of travel beginning at his home in Ephesus. He often traveled the way the mail route went from Ephesus to Smyrna, then north sixty-four miles to Pergamos, turning southeast to visit Thyatira, Sardis, Philadelphia, and Laodicea.

The number seven claims our attention. In chapter one of the Revelation, John sees seven stars in the right hand of Christ. He also pictures Christ walking in the midst of seven golden candlesticks. Seven is a number used to denote perfection or completeness. The seven stars, which are angels or ministers to the seven churches, are seen in the right hand of God. Speaking of ministers as stars, we are reminded of Daniel's words, "And they that be wise shall shine as the brightness of the firmament; and they that turn many to righteousness as the stars forever and ever" (Dan 12:3). Holding the seven stars is symbolic of God's holding all His ministers in the hand of His power. For example, when a large object is held in the hand, only part is actually touched by the fingers, but the entire object is held. This is also true of Christ walking in the midst of the seven churches. This symbolizes His presence in the midst of all congregations of the church. There were other congregations in Asia Minor, but seven is sufficient to symbolize the whole. The symbol of a candlestick or lamp is not new. John heard Jesus say, "Neither do men light a candle, and put it under a bushel, but on a candlestick; and it giveth light unto all that are in the house" (Matt. 5:15). Also, Jesus is proclaimed as the "light of the world." He further expresses to the disciples, "Ye are the light of the world" (Matt. 5:14). What oil is to a lamp, the Holy Spirit is to the church. Without it, we become only empty lamps void of light. The "golden" candlestick depicts the church as precious.

The Candlesticks

1. The Candlestick at Ephesus (Rev. 2:1-7)

Ephesus was an ancient city. It was noted as a very important commercial, political, and religious center. The Apostle Paul went to this wicked, idolatrous city and established the church. Some of the things Paul encountered have been recorded in Acts chapter 19. The temple of the goddess Diana was the greatest glory of the city. The Greeks boasted, "The sun sees nothing finer in its course than Diana's Temple."[1] One would suppose the image of Diana to be very beautiful; however, to us it would be very repulsive. The image is grotesque, ugly, and covered with many breasts, which was a symbol of fertility. The Ephesians believe it had been dropped from heaven. This temple became the shrine of heathen superstition, vileness, and immorality. It was in this city that Paul labored longer than in any other.

How great the power of the gospel to convert the heathen and plant the true church! Paul's Epistle to the Ephesians reveals an established congregation abounding in spiritual life. The glorious doctrine of sanctification is set forth as Paul writes, "And grieve not the holy Spirit of God, whereby ye are sealed unto the day of redemption" (Eph. 4:30). And again, "Christ also loved the church, and gave himself for it; that he might sanctify and cleanse it . . ." (Eph. 5:25b-26a).

But from the description in the Revelation, a drastic change has taken place in the church at Ephesus. While they are commended for their words, patience, and orthodoxy, they are lacking in Christian love. As Christ walks in their midst He cries, "Nevertheless I have somewhat against thee, because thou hast left thy first love" (Rev. 2:4). Christ requires more than good works. To preserve the pure doctrine of the Christian faith is essential, but to maintain a vital, sincere love is indispensable. All else is in vain if love is lacking. This can happen to anyone.

---

[1]Barclay, William, *Letters to the Seven Churches* (New York: Abin Press, 1957), p. 14.

When one has lost that first enthusiasm of the Christian experience, he soon becomes critical, faultfinding, censorious, and self-righteous. Our works may become acts of duty rather than service of love, but the chief demand of our Lord has never changed. He still requires, "Thou shalt love the Lord thy God with thy heart, and with all thy soul, and with all thy mind. This is the first and great commandment. And the second is like unto it, Thou shalt love thy neighbor as thyself" (Matt. 22:37-39).

Christ demanded the Ephesians to repent. The demand is no less for this generation. True repentance is not only a contrite heart and tears of remorse, but also an about-face turning. It demands action to change. Real repentance means to acknowledge guilt and turn from ungodliness. God never glosses over iniquity; He demands godly sorrow, bitter regret, and a sincere forsaking of sin before He pours out His love, grace and mercy upon men. Christ said failure to repent of the cold, indifferent spirit would mean removal of the candlestick. How sad is the picture of the church or of individuals who refuse to repent. They become lamps with no oil, desolate and empty.

There is no evidence that the Ephesians repented. Their candlestick has long since been removed. Not a vestige of the church remains where once stood an important congregation. The city itself is no more.

2. *The Candlestick at Smyrna (Rev. 2:8-11)*

Smyrna, an important city of trade and noted for its beauty, was also characterized as a great center of Caesar worship. Christians were in constant peril for refusing to worship Caesar as God. Romans believed the Pax Romana, the Roman peace, was embodied and incarnated as a spirit in the emperor. During the reign of Domitian, Caesar worship became compulsory. It was demanded that once a year every Roman citizen must burn a pinch of incense to Caesar saying, "Caesar is Lord." Refusal meant disloyalty to the government. Christians lived as sheep counted for the slaughter, never knowing when the death blow would be wielded. Furthermore, the Jews who had a synagogue in Smyrna were a constant source of agitation. They often reported the deeds of the Christians to the city officials, causing punishment or death.

It seemed almost impossible to light a candle of truth in such a mass of darkness. Yet, the message of Christ to the church in Smyrna was all commendation, without reproof. The Lord had taken note of their poverty but reminded them of their spiritual treasures. He appeared unto Christians in Smyrna as "he that was dead and is alive," and foretold a period of tribulation:

> Fear none of those things which thou shalt suffer: behold, the devil shall cast some of you into prison, that ye may be tried; and ye shall have tribulation ten days: be thou faithful unto death, and I will give thee a crown of life (Rev. 2:10).

The "devil" who cast them into prison was really the power of Satan embodied in pagan Rome. Polycarp, a disciple of John the Revelator, was the pastor of the Smyrna congregation. He was given the command to sacrifice to Caesar or be burned. While this servant of Christ perished in flames he said, "I fear not the fire that burns for a season and is quenched." Thus the martyr passed into the portals beyond. The "ten days" is used as a Greek expression to mean a short period of time, and no doubt has reference to ten years of intense persecution.

It is most interesting to note that Smyrna yet stands today. Approximately one-half of its population of 250,000 inhabitants are nominally Christian.[2] Its candle flame has never gone out although often it became very dim.

The message gleaned from the Smyrna church for us today is a firm conviction that nothing can separate us from Christ, We may face poverty, trial, tribulation or death but none of these can sever us from the love of God.

---

[2]Barclay, William, *Letters to the Seven Churches.*

For I am persuaded, that neither death, nor life, nor angels, nor principalities, nor powers, nor things present, nor things to come, nor height, nor depth, nor any other creature, shall be able to separate us from the love of God, which is in Christ Jesus our Lord (Rom. 8:38, 39).

Also, let it be noted that the crown of life is only given to those who are "faithful unto death."

3. The Candlestick at Pergamos (Rev. 2:12-17)

Pergamos, "where Satan's seat is," depicts a pagan city of heathen gods and smoking altars. To visit this city of Asia, a center of idolatry in John's day, one would observe paganism at its peak. Throngs of people press toward the temple where Aesculapius, the god of healing, is worshipped. This god is acclaimed as "savior," and the symbol of worship is a serpent. Afflicted persons are urged to bathe in the temple baths and spend the night in the temple darkness. Here there are tame, harmless snakes. If one of these snakes touches or glides over the body of a sufferer, it means the touch of god himself bringing healing.

Multitudes offer their sacrifices at the shrines of the Greek gods, Althene and Zeus. Numbers can be seen flocking to the amphitheater to view bloody spectacles in the arena. No one forgets that this is a chief center of Caesar worship. Others, also great in number, enter the temple of Venus with its licentious rites.

But not all wend their way in heathenism. There are a few, perhaps not many, of the noted or great among them, who make their way to some upper room or perhaps a cave in the mountain side. These are called followers of "the way." Their God is the Lord of all. The Christ is present in their midst and utters, "I know thy works."

The ever-seeing eye of Christ notes the good as well as the evil, but He who commends righteousness also must condemn iniquity. There were those in Pergamos who compromised the truth with idolatry. They encouraged the eating of meats sacrificed to idols and committed fornication. A reference is given of

an Old Testament story where God sent judgment on Israel when
Balak and Balaam taught the people to sin in this same manner.
God was displeased with Israel, and because of their fornication
twenty-four thousand fell in one day. (See Numbers 22 through
25 and 31:13-17.) His judgment also fell on Pergamos as He
fought against them with the "sword of his mouth." There is no
room for compromise in the religion of Christ. He taught, "No
man can serve two masters" (Matt. 6:24a). He demands complete surrender. The call still echoes for men like Antipas, the
faithful martyr. Even the price of death was not too great to pay.
"To him that overcometh will I give . . . him a white stone, and
in the stone a new name written, which no man knoweth saving
he that receiveth it" (Rev. 2:17). Christ is that hidden manna, the
Bread of Life. The white stone may refer to the ancient custom
in which votes were cast by a jury placing stones in an urn. A
black stone meant "guilty." The white stone stood for acquittal in
the day of judgment. Another custom of the heathen was the
wearing of a precious white stone as a charm. Only the wearer
knew the mystic writing on the stone which, according to tradition, was to give protection and good fortune. He who over-
comes sin receives Christ as the true and living Stone. Only the
Christian knows what it means to have His name engraved on
the heart. This name alone can keep you safe.

4. The Candlestick at Thyatira (Rev. 2:18-29)

Foes from within are always much more dangerous than
enemies from without. The threat of outward religious dangers
was less in Thyatira than in other cities of the seven churches
mentioned in the Revelation. It was not a city of noted pagan religions. Some heathen temples were there, but Caesar worship
was not pronounced. Thyatira was especially marked as a great
center of trade. We remember that Lydia, the seller of purple,
was a citizen of this city. This great commercial center was
known for its dyeing industry. Many trade guilds functioned in a
similar manner to some unions of our day; however, the Chris-

tian faced difficulty in joining the trade guilds because of evil social activities involved. The guild shared meals from meat sacrificed to idols, and wine flowed freely. Often the event would be held in the heathen temple. To refrain from attending the social function was to forfeit employment; thus, the temptation for compromise to maintain economic resources was extremely great.

While the letter to Thyatira begins with words of worthy acclaim, it soon becomes a letter of censor to those who have become the prey of compromise. A woman who calls herself a prophetess becomes the central figure of reproof. The name Jezebel alludes to a story in the Book of Kings. A wicked woman bearing this name seduced her husband, King Ahab, into idolatry. In like manner, this Jezebel of Thyatira was seducing the church into idolatrous living, eating meats sacrificed to idols and committing adultery. Some say she was the pastor's wife. Others believe she served as the minister. In any measure, she was a powerful influence for evil in the congregation. For the church to tolerate this iniquity meant to share in her punishment. God gave time for repentance and now judgment would be brought.

Truth is ever the same. Inward foes of evil cause decay and death more rapidly than outward foes of persecution. The longest letter of the seven is written to this church with the least outward danger. He who comes with "eyes of flaming fire" cautions man of harbored sin within.

5. The Candlestick at Sardis (Rev. 3:1-6)

Sardis, one of the oldest cities in the world, boasted of wealth, pleasure, and luxury. The first coins minted in Asia Minor came from this center of riches. The once militant city now rested nonchalantly in the memories of past achievements. Citizens of Sardis became mad with wealth, intoxicated with pleasure, and trusted in materialism.

Instead of the church influencing people of Sardis to become spiritually awakened, it, too, fell asleep. Their slumber became the sleep of death. There was no great danger here from persecution. Even the Jews gave little protest; neither were they troubled with false doctrine in the church. Lulled to sleep in the bed of complacency, the church became unconscious of her opportunities, responsibilities, and even dangers.

Soldiers of this once militant church fastened their polished Christian armors securely, laid aside their helmets of salvation, and fell asleep. The truth girt about their loins was silent; the breastplate of righteousness became only a form of religion; feet once shod with peace toward God and man became peace with sin and Satan. Shields of faith and swords of the spirit lay within their reach—but they were asleep. With their heads in the lap of the world, they were shorn of their power like Samson in Delilah's web. When Satan puts a church to sleep, the victory is in his hands.

There are those who rest in a doctrine of eternal security, believing they can never be lost after once knowing Christ. Here was a church once in fellowship with our Lord, not even charged with heresy or works of iniquity. Yet they had become as dead branches, bearing no fruit, and were cut off the vine and burned. Once alive, now they were dead! Too many are as foolish virgins, still carrying empty lamps that were once aflame. Now, sleeping so soundly, they hear not the voice, "Awake thou that sleepest, and arise from the dead, and Christ shall give thee light" (Eph. 5 :14). Christ gave Sardis the warning, "thou shalt not know what hour I will come upon thee" (Rev. 3:3). In a world of drowsy saints and sleeping sinners let us heed the command, "Watch therefore, for ye know neither the day nor the hour wherein the Son of man cometh" (Matt. 25:13).

6. The Candlestick at Philadelphia (Rev. 3:7-13)

Undiluted praise for the church at Philadelphia flowed from the lips of the one ". . . that is holy, he that is true, he that hath the key of David, he that openeth, and no man shutteth; and shutteth, and no man openeth" (Rev. 3:7). Praise without blame is to be greatly coveted. With keen interest, the church at Philadelphia is viewed to discover the virtues which merit this tribute offered by Christ.

"I know thy works," said Christ. Worthy praise is not given without faithful labor. More people will appear on Christ's left hand on the day of judgment because of the sin of omission than for willfully committed transgressions. In Christ's picture of the judgment there is a listing of deeds people did not do which caused them to be lost (Matt. 25:41-46). Many miss the commendation of our Lord because of prayers they leave unuttered, service they will not give, commandments they refuse to keep, tithes they will not render, and souls they fail to win. The Philadelphia congregation is also commended for its loyalty in keeping the Word of Christ and not denying His name. This is evidence of their sincere love for Jesus. "He that hath my commandments, and keepeth them, he it is that loveth me" (John 14:21a). Not denying His name is to identify ourselves with Christ in holiness, doctrine, and spirit.

A door is a means of entrance or escape. Christ is the Open Door offered to the loyal church. Jesus said, "I am the door" (John 10:7-9). Ancient shepherds stood at the opening in the wall and counted the sheep as they passed through. The shepherd then lay down across the opening and became the only door. Only through Christ may we gain entrance to heaven. But this "open door" is more. It is the door to opportunities for greater service, richer experiences and missionary endeavor.

Geographically, Philadelphia was the gateway to the East. Through this border town many travelers passed to the country beyond. Christ points out that He is the only "gateway" to the heavenly city.

A door is also a means of escape. Only those who enter through Christ escape eternal destruction. Good works and loyalty are to be rewarded. The overcomer is made a pillar in God's temple, the church.

7. The Candlestick at Laodicea (Rev. 3:14-22)

Laodiceans, proud and haughty, sought no help from God or man. Boasting of riches, they were unaware of the truth that God saw them as paupers. This center of commerce gloried in having the chief banking arrangements for all Asia Minor. Their clothing industry produced the finest wool and most costly garments. Yet Christ, the faithful and true Witness, revealed naked souls without white raiment. They had well-adorned the outer man but had given the inner man little concern.

Laodicea was noted as a healing center, famous for its baths and medical school. It produced medicines for the physical eyes, but the blind eyes of their souls remained in darkness. The god of materialism reigned and spiritual help was unsought. How deplorable the state of the individual, church, or nation that endeavors to succeed without God.

The striking comparison between Laodicea of Asia Minor and the Laodiceans of the twentieth century is too close for comfort. Our materialistic world must learn that money may buy houses, but not homes; science may produce medicines but not health; nuclear weapons may exert power but fail to bring peace; religious formality may salve the conscience, but only true salvation can save the soul.

Multitudes still seek for a middle path, neither for nor against Christ. Desiring to be only lukewarm, they have forgotten His words, "He that is not with me is against me" (Matt. 12:30). Yet, how great is the love of God, that He stands so long knocking at the door of man's heart. His mercy is extended even to those who merit no words of commendation. Of Ephesus it could be said that they were not wanting in works. Even of Sardis it was expressed that there were a few who had not defiled their garments. But Christ had nothing to commend in Laodicea. It is beyond human comprehension that He should desire to enter their hearts or ours, and "sup" with them or us.

These seven candles seem to portray seven consecutive stages of Christianity. Ephesus symbolizes first-century Christians who left their first love and drifted into apostasy. Smyrna's tribulations mark the death of saints during an age of martyrs. Pergamos depicts the period of compromise when the Christian faith was compromised with Roman Catholicism. Thyatira is an example of the apostasy at the darkest period of the Dark Ages. Sardis tells of spiritual death that reigned until the candle of the sixteenth century became aflame as it is observed in the church at Philadelphia. It is significant that the two candles with flames that were not extinguished are those representing the martyrs and reformers; their light burns eternally! In this Laodicean day may God help us to see that nominal Christianity is neither hot nor cold. It is poor, wretched, naked and blind.

Centuries have passed since the admonition of Christ was sent to the seven churches. All that remains of Ephesus is a gigantic heap of ruins. Its only marking now is a Turkish village of Ayassoluk. Pergamos and Thyatira no longer remain to boast of their many gods and smoking altars. Sardis has passed out of existence. The stately theaters, the bank, and the circus of Laodicea are now inhabited with foxes, wolves, and serpents. As though by divine providence of God, Smyrna and Philadelphia alone remain with a candlestick of Christianity.

John Writes a Preface Page (Rev. 4—5)

The author's introduction set the stage for the great drama of prophecy which follows. It is understood that the Apocalypse is not a single vision but a *series* of symbolic revelations.

Prophecy does not begin in the last book of the Bible but in the first book, Genesis. Events of the Old Testament are as a roll of picture film, negatives or shadow pictures (Heb. 10:1), with little meaning unless they are held to the light given in the New Testament. John skillfully takes the vague forms, types and shadows, holds them to Christ, the Light, then produces the developed pictures. The central theme of the whole Bible is the redemption of man through Jesus Christ. To introduce this theme in the Revelation, John chooses one of the oldest scenes of Jewish worship, the encampment of the Israelites in the wilderness.

Under the influence of the spirit of prophecy, John is carried away in his vision to the throne of God. Jews believed that worship in heaven was conducted in much the same manner as in the pattern given to Moses. The ark of the covenant was a symbol of God's throne. Here God met with man. In spirit, John stands in awe before the Omnipotent One. He who sits upon the throne as a "jasper and a sardine stone." These stones of exuberant brilliance—the jasper as a diamond, the sardine as stones of glistening red hue—depict vestments of a great Monarch. Jews defined the dazzling light as the Shekinah. There is no description of God Himself as to form or dimension. God cannot be symbolized because there is no analogous object to compare with Him. The throne is a symbol of His supreme power and authority. A radiance of emerald clearness forms a rainbow around the throne. The rainbow was no doubt a perfect one, a complete circle as ours would be if it were all visible. It is the symbol of God's covenant. Like the circle, it has no end.

When John tells of twenty-four elders around the throne, he gives reference to the twenty-four courses of Jewish priests dwelling in tents next to the tabernacle. The New Testament Church is God's tabernacle of today (Eph. 2:22). John merges the two dispensations into one—type and antitype, prophecy and fulfillment. The twenty-four elders of John's vision are the twelve patriarchs the natural heads of the tribes of Israel, and the twelve apostles, the spiritual leaders of the New Testament Church. Paul also gives reference to this truth: "And are built upon the foundation of the apostles and prophets, Jesus Christ himself being the chief cornerstone" (Eph. 2:20).

The "lightnings, thunderings, and voices" heard by John are usual manifestations of God's presence as expressed in Old Testament times. John's mentioning of the seven lamps of fire gives reference to the golden candlestick of the temple. The laver of the temple court answers to the "sea of glass, like unto crystal."

To understand the sublime imagery employed by John's vision of beasts, full of eyes, like a lion, a calf, a man's face, and a flying eagle, it is necessary to recall visions of Ezekiel (Ezek. 1:5-14) and Isaiah (Isa. 6:1-13). "Beasts," before and behind the throne of God, sounds very crude. The translation of the word "beast" is inaccurate. The original word is "zoon," which signifies "a living creature."[3] Many translators use this more correct rendering. When Ezekiel saw these four living creatures in his vision, they were as familiar to him as the American flag, a golden eagle, or the Statue of Liberty would be to an American. He understood that the twelve tribes of Israel were divided into four major divisions, each bearing its own insignia. The "lion" was the emblem for Judah of the eastern division with the two other tribes, Issachar and Zabulon, Ephraim, along with Manasseh and Benjamin, formed the western division and chose the calf or ox symbol.

According to the Rabbins, the standard for Reuben, whose tents were pitched with Gad and Simeon on the south, was "the face of a man." Dan of the north division, with Asher and Naphtali chose as their insignia the "flying eagle."[4] As the four major divisions of Israel are all-inclusive, whole and complete, symbolically, they represent the entire church of God in the gospel dispensation—saints from all four quarters of the earth worshipping at God's throne. John's vision later includes the song of this redeemed host proclaiming, "for thou wast slain, and hast redeemed us to God by thy blood out of every kindred, and tongue, and people, and nation" (Rev. 5:9).

Much of the phraseology John used is rabbinical. Isaiah saw symbolic visions of living creatures with six wings, long before John wrote the Apocalypse. The rabbis explain this metaphor was used to express the solemnity of being in the presence of the Almighty. With two wings the living creatures cover their eyes lest they should behold the countenance of the Deity; with two wings they cover their feet lest they should touch His foot-

---

[3]Smith, F. G., *Revelation Explained*, p. 53.
[4]Adam Clarke, *Commentary*, Vol. VI, p. 989.

stool; with two wings they fly in adoration to sanctify His great Name. Holy to the Father, Holy to the Son, Holy to the Spirit; this is the refrain of heavenly worship which is never silent day or night.

To depict God as "Sovereign," living creatures are selected from all forms of life. Man, the highest intellectual creature; lion, king of beasts; calf or ox, chief among cattle; and the eagle, king of birds; all are pictured at His feet. "Let everything that hath breath praise the Lord" (Ps. 150:6).

According to Christian tradition, these four creatures refer to the four evangelists, the authors of the Gospels. The "lion" is attributed to Mark and indicates a bold, courageous character. The "calf" expresses the sacrificial nature of Luke's writing. Matthew is assigned the creature "as the face of a man," denoting wisdom and intelligence. The flying "eagle," the bird that soars the highest and gazes directly into the sun, is ascribed to John, revealing strength to rise above earthly obstacles. While it is no doubt true that the evangelists personally possessed these worthy attributes, it is much more notable to observe their writings reveal the perfection of these characteristics in the Christ. These virtues—wisdom, sacrifice, courage, and strength—must also be evident in the church, which is His body.

The attention of John is attracted to a book in the right hand of the Deity upon the throne. The book is sealed with seven seals. A strong angel appears calling with a loud voice for someone to open the book. When no one in heaven or earth is found worthy to loose the seals, John weeps. This scene of God seated on a literal throne with a book in His hand must be regarded as an accommodation to the human mind for comprehending infinite things scaled down to human understanding.

The book, which is in God's right hand of power, symbolizes God's plan of redemption through all ages. In scroll form, seven pieces of parchment individually sealed express a complete book, completely sealed. Even Gabriel could not bring to the world a revelation of God's plan. Remember the Scripture

DANIEL STRIP

passage, "which things the angels desired to look into" (1 Pet. 1:10-12). Neither could Moses nor the prophets unveil the hidden plan. John's weeping ceases when one of the elders exclaims, "Weep not: behold, the Lion of the tribe of Judah, the Root of David, hath prevailed to open the book, and to loose the seals thereof" (Rev. 5:5).

No one but Christ, God's own Son, was found worthy to declare Him. ". . . the only begotten Son, which is in the bosom of the Father, he hath declared him" (John 1:18). Christ is born of the tribe of Judah whose insignia is the "lion." Here the courage, strength, and power of Christ is depicted. "Root of David" refers to the lineage of Christ's ancestors in the flesh.

Appearing in the midst of the throne is a slain lamb with seven horns and seven eyes. To reveal God's plan of redemption required more than the courage and power of a "lion." It demanded the sacrifice of a "lamb." Only through death, through the giving of life's blood, could Christ reveal the Father's plan to save the world. Seven is a symbolic number appearing in the Revelation indicative of completeness or perfection. God has seemingly written the number in the natural world with seven basic colors of the rainbow. There are only seven. All shades are drawn from blending these. It is also written in the world of sound. There are seven basic notes of music. All harmony, major and minor refrains, are made from compositions of these seven basic notes. It then becomes easy to understand John's use of "seven" in the Scriptures. The slain Lamb having seven horns bids a search for the meaning of "horn." It is written in Psalm 18:2, "The Lord is my rock . . . and the horn of my salvation." This means the Lord is the "power of my salvation." Again, there is the Scripture reference to Christ, "And hath raised up an horn of salvation for us in the house of his servant David" (Luke 1:69). Seven horns, therefore, would mean complete power as He uttered, "All power is given unto me in heaven and in earth" (Matt. 28:18). Seven eyes convey the thought of complete insight and all knowledge. The great song of redemption echoes through heaven's courts as all creatures worship, praise, and adore the Lamb of God.

A Table of Contents (Rev. 6)

The register of chapter headings indicates subjects to be treated in the book proper. John lists topics, giving the reader a glimpse of what may be anticipated in chapters to follow. Chapter headings are never complete in themselves, but simply introduce the themes to be considered. The author presents his topics in the opening of the book sealed with seven seals. It has already been established that John's prophecies cover the scope between Christ's first and second coming. It may be observed that the sixth seal opening depicts the second coming of Christ. It is therefore logical to place the opening of the first seal at the first advent of our Lord.

(See Picture Chart following page 32: Strip 1)

1. Opening the first seal (Rev. 6:1-2) presents a symbol used by the Romans to portray a conqueror. John sees a white horse having a rider with a bow, going forth to conquer. To interpret Biblical symbols the key is to find the symbol elsewhere in the scriptures. The story of the flood in Noah's day gives the sign of God's promise by a rainbow. The rainbow is a complete circle. We see only half of it because of the horizon. John's vision depicts a promise in the hand of the conqueror as a bow. The promise is victory through God's Word and the arrow is the Spirit. Since the author's subject is religion and the chronological placement of the seal vision is at Christ's first advent, we immediately direct our thinking to our Lord who introduced to the world the mighty, aggressive religion of pure **Christianity.** The symbol drawn from militant life is not a new metaphor. Paul also speaks of soldiers of Jesus Christ (2 Tim. 2:3-4). Christ established a militant church with power to conquer all her foes. New Testament Christians marched boldly to war against sin under the banner of the cross. This book of prophecy follows the

trail of human blood throughout the centuries, across many fields of battle, but claims ultimate victory for Christ and His church.

2. Hearts are made to tremble at the opening of the second seal (Rev. 6:3-4). Here is a horse of red whose rider carries a great sword to kill. The forward march of Christ's militant church was not to be unchallenged. As soon as Christianity attained prominence in the Roman Empire, supporters of pagan religions increased opposition. Heathen temples were being abandoned as people learned of the true God. Paganism would not be conquered without many casualties. **Pagan Rome,** rider of the red horse, exerted her state authority to slaughter multiplied thousands of Christians. The sword to kill and the color of red are descriptive of the cruelty, murder, and bloodshed by pagan powers. This chapter heading excites interest in chapters following which describe in fuller detail the conflict between Christianity and Pagan Rome.

3. Opening the third seal (Rev. 6:5-6), there is seen a horse of black. The rider is seen with a pair of balances in his hand and he is weighing food.

As soon as Christianity had conquered paganism, another force of evil began to appear on the field of battle. It is well known that when old Pagan Rome fell, a new Rome began to take form. Pagan Rome bequeathed her nature, power, and authority to the new empire. Constantine, the first Christian emperor, made Christianity the state religion. Thus multitudes took on forms of Christianity without any change of heart. This produced a pagan Rome in a Christian garb. Persecution of Christians ceased and many believers relaxed into complacency; thus, the result was an apostasy. Early beginnings of this were evident in John's day. He saw the darkness approaching as the candlesticks were removed from the churches of Asia Minor. The apostasy (the falling away from truth) gave birth to a Papal Rome. People no longer worshipped gods and demi-gods as pagans, but worshipped the Virgin Mary and the saints. They did not burn incense to the emperor as a god, but esteemed the pope as supreme head of the church. The contrast between a white and black horse delineates the transition from gospel light to spiritual darkness.

Balances to weigh and measure food depict a symbol of famine. Amos, the prophet, foretells in the Old Testament, "Behold, the days come, saith the Lord God, that I will send a famine in the land, not a famine of bread, nor a thirst for water, but of hearing the words of the Lord" (Amos 8:11). John describes a spiritual famine in Rev. 6:6. Repeatedly "oil" is used in the scripture to signify the Holy Spirit. Wheat is to depict bread, God's Word. Souls were starved for spiritual food.

This was fulfilled when the Roman church denied the Scriptures, the Bread of Life, to souls starved for truth. Papal Rome endeavored to destroy true Christianity with the sword, fire and dungeon. But truth is destined to conquer; the Papal Rome that ruled the world was dethroned and true Christians were free from their bondage.

4. Opening of the fourth seal (Rev. 6:7-8) brings a pale horse to view. The rider is labeled "Death." When Papal Rome lost her supremacy, the great Reformation restored much of the truth buried during the Dark Ages. The true church emerged from seclusion and the restoration of gospel light began. Because many Christians now boldly protested teaching of Catholic Rome, they were called "Protestants"; thus, **Protestantism** was born. How sad is the fact that many of the errors of Catholicism were carried over into the Protestant faith. Rome believed in a state religion and compelled all people to bow to her commands. It is deplorable that Luther gave to Germany a state church; Zwingli introduced a state church to Switzerland; John Knox established state religion in Scotland; and King Henry VIII founded the Church of England. In many other ways Protestantism is a mixture of truth and Catholic error. A "pale horse," not "white" like the New Testament church, is symbolized; neither "black" as Catholicism is depicted, but a mixture of black and white—this is Protestantism. Soon after Protestantism was

born, it became a cold, formal body interested largely in strict, formal laws. We recall sincere Christians, called Puritans and Pilgrims, coming to America in search of religious freedom. Their persecution in England and Europe was not at the hands of Catholic power but from the Protestant State Church. Early Protestantism is also guilty of the bloodshed of many Christians who refused to bow to her commands.

The rider is not named "Death" because of the physical slaughter alone, but because it is indicative of the spiritual extinction of life, prevalent in the Protestant body.

5. Opening the fifth seal (Rev. 6:9-11), there is a complete change of symbols. The preceding chapter headings indicated that the true church would be engaged in spiritual conflict against evil forces. Many Christians would suffer death in battle. Like the blood of Abel crying from the ground, Gen. 4:10, the cries of the martyr's blood ascended to God's throne. Now John is carried in spirit to the throne of God to behold the souls of the martyrs who were slain in spiritual warfare. Here is an explicit contrast. While saints were being killed on earth, they were being honored in heaven. God was not asleep when men and women died for His name. To suffer with Him meant to reign with Him (2 Tim. 2:12).

John's vision reveals the souls under the altar—under the blood and sacrifice of Christ. These martyrs desired avenging judgment on those who persecuted Christians on earth. They were rewarded with white robes and bidden to rest until the prophecy should be fulfilled that others would be slain as they had been. We may rightfully use the topic "The Reign of the Martyrs" for a chapter heading in the Table of Contents.

6. Opening the sixth seal (Rev. 6:12-17), the scene abruptly changes again. John beholds a mighty earthquake, the heavens departing as a scroll, all men standing at the seat of judgment, many crying for rocks and mountains to fall on them. Speaking of earthquakes, the world of our day is now experiencing such a state of chaos. There is a political eruption shaking every con-

tinent of the earth. Where once solid ground provided secure foundations for freedom, we find trembling sand. An economical earthquake is as a volcano bursting into every level of society. Scientifically, our world is in a mass of confusion racing for other planets. Socially, the uprisings of various races, classes, and castes present serious problems. Morally, standards of chaste living are being tossed aside, resulting in crime, divorce, and mental, physical, and spiritual disease. Materialism has blinded the eyes of multitudes who build life's houses on the sinking sand. They are giving no thought to spiritual values. Religiously, the earthquake makes its mark as millions are lost in the shuffle of disconcerting beliefs. All these are but a prelude to the earthquake of the last great day.

We have read of God's judgment with fire and brimstone on Sodom and Gomorrah; we have read of the antediluvian world being destroyed by flood, and of the destruction of Jerusalem. Many other examples of His wrath may be recalled but nothing is to be compared with the "great day of his wrath" at Christ's second coming.

THE GREAT JUDGMENT MORNING

I dreamed that the great judgment morning
Had dawned, and the trumpet had blown;
I dreamed that the nations had gathered
To judgment before the white throne;
From the throne came a bright shining angel
And stood on the land and the sea,
And swore with his hand raised to heaven,
That time was no longer to be.

The rich man was there, but his money
Had melted and vanished away;
A pauper he stood in the judgment,
His debts were too heavy to pay:
The great man was there, but his greatness
When death came was left far behind;
The angel that opened the records,
Not a trace of his greatness could find.

The moral man came to the judgment,
But his self-righteous rags would not do;
The men who had crucified Jesus
Had passed off as moral men, too;
The souls that had put off salvation—
"Not tonight; I'll get saved by-and-by;
No time now to think of religion!"
At last they had found time to die.

And oh, what a weeping and wailing,
As the lost were told of their fate:
They cried for the rocks and the mountains,
They prayed, but their prayer was too late.[5]

7. Opening the seventh seal (Rev. 8), the author lists an Appendix or Summary to the Table of Contents. Under the symbols of this seal, the subject matter is traced again with the sounding of seven trumpets. All things come to a final consummation as the note of the last trumpet sounds.

_____

[5]*Clayton Choir Melodies*—#1 (Indiana: The Rodeheaver Hall-Mack Company), p. 57. Used by permission.

CHAPTER II

THE KEY TO THE SYMBOLS

Keys—how important they are! There are small and large ones, with various sizes in between. Some keys are composed of metal, others are of wood or plastic. Numerals, colors, combinations, figures, or words also serve as keys. Without keys treasury vaults remain closed, automobiles make no motion, doors remain shut, maps fail to have meaning, and all intelligible thought is only a puzzle; even life itself is but a strange enigma.

When John first saw the Christ on Patmos Isle, his attention was drawn to the keys that hung from the Master's golden girdle. The Lord explained these were "the keys of hell and of death" (Rev. 1:18). A father once stood with his minister observing the mortician turn the key sealing the vault which would soon be planted in the earth. The mortician explained, "I will leave the key in the care of the sexton." Tears flowed from the father's eyes as he walked toward the cemetery gate. Consolation came as the minister said, "Christ has the key to all these graves, and on the resurrection morning He will turn every lock of death. The brown blanket of earth will be tossed aside and your little girl will rise as a beautiful flower of spring. Christ is the true Keeper of the keys."

Our troubled world has searched for the key to peace. It has tried the keys of science, politics, education, and numerous others only to find they fail to bring the desired peace and happiness. Only Christ has such a key, for He holds the key to life as well as the key of death.

Christ is also the key of the Scriptures. As the letters of the alphabet are important to language, Christ is the Alpha and Omega of the holy writings. Without Christ neither history or prophecy have meaning. He is the key to the future, and heaven is locked until the Divine Key opens its portals. The Word of God provides the key to the symbols of prophecy.

Without a key John's visions of a seven-headed dragon, a ten horned beast, a woman standing on the moon, and many other strange characters are only as a mass of unintelligible enigmas. A literal interpretation of characters which one may expect to see in mythology or fairy tales is not only absurd but impossible.

The language of symbols is not new. Long before there was a written language of words, a system of hieroglyphics or picture language was used to convey thought. Many prophets wrote in this manner. Two books of our Bible have been labeled "apocalyptic literature" because their authors wrote in the veiled language of symbols to reveal truth which would not be known otherwise. The Book of Daniel, the first of these two books, appears in the Old Testament and was written centuries prior to the Revelation, the second apocalyptic book. It is most significant to observe the likeness of characters, style, and language used by the two authors. The most thrilling thing is that God interpreted the visions of Daniel, thus, giving the key for understanding the Revelation. God, Himself, gave the key for Revelation long before it was ever written! The reason this book has suffered much erroneous, weird speculation is the failure of interpreters to use the God-given key.

We remember school days, and that our school books included problems, and solutions in the front pages. Here a method was given for securing the correct answers. To ignore this was to fail in solving the problems which appeared later in the book. The Book of Daniel is the primer in which God gives a method of interpretation, to instruct the reader how he may calculate correct answers in the symbolic understanding of the Revelation. To better understand, let us look at God's interpretation of:

The Great Image of Daniel (Dan. 2)

During the days of Israel's captivity in Babylon, God expressed divine providence and love by the presence of a prophet, Daniel, in their midst. Nebuchadnezzar, the Babylonian king, was deeply troubled by a dream he could not remember. Wise men, astrologers, magicians, and soothsayers were all unable to reveal the dream or its meaning. It was then that Daniel and his companions, Hananiah, Mishael, and Azariah, had a prayer meeting. God revealed the dream to Daniel in a night vision.

Standing before Nebuchadnezzar, Daniel acknowledged the true God of heaven who alone knows all things. There had been a great image of a man perfectly proportioned in the dream. The head was of gold, the arms were of silver, the belly and thighs of brass, the legs of iron, and the feet were a mixture of iron and clay. Daniel explained that the image represented a succession of four universal kingdoms.

1. The golden head was a symbol of Nebuchadnezzar and the Babylonian Kingdom. It was the first universal empire. This king ruled as an absolute monarch, and many mighty deeds are attributed to him. Nebuchadnezzar was deeply interested in architecture, arts and sciences, philosophy and religion. He believed it was impossible for any nation to conquer Babylon. The high massive walls, many observation towers, and numbers of guards brought a feeling of security to him. Nebuchadnezzar built a great temple with many decorations of pure gold. Inside the temple stood a golden table where a golden image of the god Bel or Marduk stood. It is said that the solid gold table and image weighed fifty thousand pounds. Golden lions and figures of gold were also found in fifty-three other temples of Bel and at the 180 altars of Ishtar. No wonder Babylon was called the "City of Gold."

Daniel dared to tell this mighty king, who reigned from 606 to 561 B.C., that there was an end prophesied for Babylon. All earthly kings must be humbled to realize that there is a God in heaven to whom they are accountable. Daniel foretold the falling of the golden head on the image into the arms of silver, the Medo-Persian Kingdom.

2. Darius, the Median, and Cyrus, the Persian, joined their arms of military strength to capture the golden head of Babylon in 538 B.C. The perfection of the symbols is evident in marking a twofold kingdom by two arms. As silver is inferior to gold, the Medo-Persian Kingdom was inferior to Babylon.

Belshazzar became king of Babylon at Nebuchadnezzar's death. He was extremely ambitious and set a goal of one thousand provinces to belong to the Babylonian empire. When the goal was realized, a great banquet was held. Soldiers were given a holiday; guards were off duty to join the celebration; all leaders of Babylon were in one great assembly; wine flowed freely as dancing went into full swing. Then suddenly at midnight, the Medes and Persians made their attack. The Euphrates River had been diverted into another channel which gave them entrance by way of the riverbed; thus, fell mighty Babylon!

How true is the fact that nations established with a sword also will perish by the sword. It was not prophesied that the arms should hold the empire forever. Medo-Persia had great military power, science experts, educational directors, and skilled engineers. But all this could not guarantee security. The time allotted to any nation is measured by its attitude toward God. Thus, the prophecy foretold that the arms of silver would drop the kingdom of Medo-Persia into the brass lap of the Grecian Empire.

3. Alexander the Great was a fearless young man when he conquered the world of his day in 331 B.C. His father, Philip of Macedon, had established the Macedonian Empire, later referred to as the Grecian Kingdom. Alexander, an exceptionally brilliant scholar, was interested in science, philosophy, the arts, architecture, sports, and world power. As a youth he became a fearless soldier. When he had conquered the world, he desired to spread Greek culture everywhere. Greek language, dress, philosophy, architectural styles, and games became the way of life forced on all nations. Having reached his goal to conquer the world, Alexander wept because there were no more worlds to conquer. In his passion for world power he had completely ignored a search for

The Great Image of Daniel

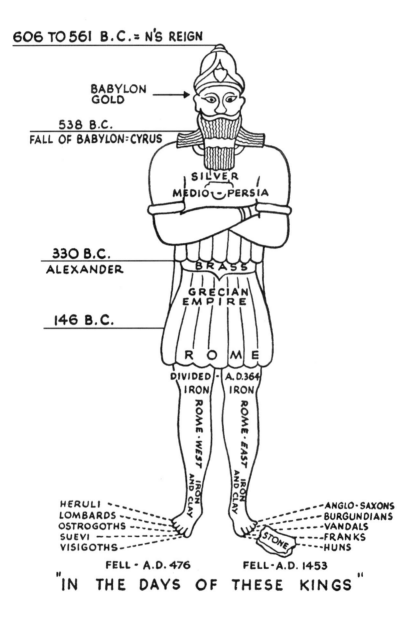

606 TO 561 B.C. = N'S REIGN

BABYLON
GOLD

538 B.C.
FALL OF BABYLON=CYRUS

SILVER
MEDIO-PERSIA

330 B.C.
ALEXANDER

BRASS

GRECIAN
EMPIRE

146 B.C.

ROME

DIVIDED - A.D.364
IRON   IRON

ROME·WEST   ROME·EAST
IRON AND CLAY   IRON AND CLAY

HERULI ----
LOMBARDS ----
OSTROGOTHS ----
SUEVI -----
VISIGOTHS ----

---- ANGLO·SAXONS
---- BURGUNDIANS
----VANDALS
----FRANKS
----HUNS

STONE

FELL - A.D. 476   FELL - A.D. 1453

"IN THE DAYS OF THESE KINGS"

the power of self-control. He became a victim of his own sinful vices and died at the age of thirty-three as a slave to passion and strong drink. How true the words of the wise man, "He that is slow to anger is better than the mighty; and he that ruleth his spirit than he that taketh a city" (Prov. 16:32).

At the death of Alexander, his kingdom was divided among four selfish kings. The kingdom became weak and soon fell at the feet of Rome in 146 B.C. However, Greek culture, learning, philosophy, and language survived. These still hold a part in the world of our day.

4. The legs of iron on the great image seen in the vision symbolized the Roman Empire. Again, two parts expressed the division of east and west Rome. The ten toes denoted the ten kingdoms to appear late in Rome's history. This was the last of the four universal kingdoms. The prophecies never depict any more kingdoms with such universal dominion.

Rome reached its zenith of power through Augustus Caesar, under whose rule the Lord Jesus Christ was born. Here the prophecy is fulfilled, "And in the days of these kings shall the God of heaven set up a kingdom, which shall never be destroyed: and the kingdom shall not be left to other people, but it shall break in pieces and consume all these kingdoms, and it shall stand for ever" (Dan. 2:44).

God's footprint is visible in every age of history. As nations rise and crumble, God is confidently accomplishing His divine purposes. When God's chosen Israel failed to obey Him, He allowed Babylon to carry them away into captivity. Here they learned the lessons of obedience, humility, and dependence upon God. Under Medo-Persian dominion, Israel became more perfectly fashioned by the tools of oppression and suffering. Through the Grecian Empire, God established a universal language providing a vehicle to carry the gospel of His kingdom to all people. By means of the Pax Romana, the Roman peace, God maneuvered the plans of men to fulfill His design of preparation for the establishment of His kingdom of peace. Rome provided means of communication, roads of travel, and a sense of a universal kingdom. These contributions prepared the way for the gospel to be carried to all nations, and made ready the minds of men to comprehend a cosmic King ruling a universal kingdom.

God has had a purpose for every nation since time began. Our America is not without divine destiny. Her place in the sun will be determined by the manner in which she fulfills God's design. America must also learn the lessons of obedience, humility and dependence upon God. It will either be "this nation under God," or become a nation under the heel of a dictator, domestic or foreign born. Must we be fashioned by the tools of oppression and suffering at the hands of Godless nations? Dr. Louis Evans, in his excellent book entitled *This Is America's Hour,* makes the following statements: "America needs a rebirth of the spirit if she is to maintain world leadership. Communism is challenging us to outlive it with Christianity. It is the power of the cross against the propaganda of the sickle. We must not only outpromise the Communists; we must outpassion them. We must teach our youth the concepts of the Kingdom of God with greater earnestness and thoroughness than the Kremlin teaches its youth."[1] The hour to declare the kingdom of God is now!

The great image is given for a background to make a striking comparison between the kingdoms of men and the kingdom of God.

5. The stone cut out of the mountain without hands now claims full attention.

"Forasmuch as thou sawest that the stone was cut out of the mountain without hands, and that it brake in pieces the iron, the brass, the clay, the silver, and the gold; the great God hath made known to the king what shall come to pass hereafter" (Dan. 2:45).

Here is the focal point of the prophecy. The universal kingdoms of men fall one by one but God's kingdom is universal and

---

[1]Evans, Louis H., *This is America's Hour* (Fleming H. Revell Co., Westwood, N.J.), p.38.

will never be destroyed (Dan. 2:44). Earthly kingdoms are of earthly origin but God's kingdom is divine and of heavenly birth. It is important to observe the time God set to lay a foundation for his kingdom. It is written, "In the days of these kings" (Dan. 2:44a). This stone strikes the image on the feet, the last of the universal kingdoms; thus, Christ is born in the days of the Roman Empire.

Christ is this "stone." This is a fulfillment of God's Word. "Therefore thus saith the Lord God, Behold, I lay in Zion for a foundation a stone, a tried stone, a precious corner stone, a sure foundation" (Isa. 28:16a). Christ Himself claimed to be this stone. "Jesus saith unto them, Did ye never read in the scriptures, The stone which the builders rejected, the same is become the head of the corner: this is the Lord's doing, and it is marvelous in our eyes? Therefore say I unto you, the kingdom of God shall be taken from you, and given to a nation bringing forth the fruits thereof. And whosoever shall fall on this stone shall be broken: but on whomsoever it shall fall, it will grind him to powder" (Matt. 21:42-44).

Jesus is this Stone cut out of the mountain of humanity without hands. He came by divine virgin birth; man had no part in His coming. Christ is our Solid Rock, the Rock of Ages. This foundation for the kingdom was laid at Christ's first advent. The prophet Isaiah foretells that the kingdom would come when He came as a child. "For unto us a child is born, unto us a son is given: and the government shall be upon his shoulder: . . . of the increase of his government . . . there shall be no end" (Isa. 9:6-7). Many are looking for Christ to do, at His second advent, that which He already did at His first coming. Scriptural evidence is abundant to proclaim that Christ established His Kingdom at His first coming. John the Baptist prepared the way for Christ's message with the call to "Repent ye: for the kingdom of heaven is at hand" (Matt. 3:2). This text was repeated by the Lord Himself at the beginning of His ministry (Matt. 4:17). Mark records the Master's words explaining when the kingdom would come saying, "Verily I say unto you, That there be some of them that stand here, which shall not taste of death, till they have seen the kingdom of God come with power" (Mark 9:1). Luke inscribes the Lord saying, "The law and the prophets were until John: since that time the kingdom of God is preached, and every man presseth into it" (Luke 16:16). The Apostle John declares he was "in the kingdom and patience of Jesus Christ" (Rev. 1:9). This same writer tells how we enter the kingdom by a new birth (John 3:5).

To those who desire to make Peter the rock foundation of the church, it is well to let Peter speak for himself. There is no question that Peter believed that Christ is the foundation stone:

"To whom coming, as unto a living stone, disallowed indeed of men, but chosen of God, and precious, . . . Wherefore also it is contained in the scripture, Behold I lay in Zion a chief corner stone, elect, precious . . ." (1 Pet. 2:4-8). It is noted that Peter makes reference to the prophecy in Isaiah 28:16. (See also Acts 4:9-12.)

How true the prophecy is that this stone would smite the image, cause it to fall, and carry it away as the winds blow the chaff on a summer threshing floor. All the universal kingdoms of men have passed away; but God's kingdom is the stone which becomes a mountain to fill the whole earth. The stone laid in Zion becomes Mount Zion, the peak of truth.

The kingdom of God is a sublime, vast subject. No one set of symbols could begin to express its multiple phases. This may be noted when Christ used many parables to explain the nature of the kingdom. The thirteenth chapter of Matthew alone contains seven parables descriptive of the kingdom. The same fact is true when symbols are used. They present a number of parallel themes to reveal a more comprehensive description of God's kingdom. Daniel presents the kingdom of God in contrast with earthly empires, by a number of symbolic themes. In addition to the image in the Book of Daniel, let us observe one more set of symbols so that we may better understand this type of language.

Daniel's Vision of the Four Beasts (Dan. 7)

(See Picture Chart following page 32)

Daniel's vision of the metallic image depicted four earthly kingdoms. The vision of the four beasts portray the nature of the four kings governing their domains. Forty-eight years elapsed between the dream of the metallic image and Daniel's vision of four strange beasts. In the night hours Daniel saw a vision of a tempestuous sea out of which four beasts arose. The beasts were all different. The first was as a lion with eagle's wings; the second was like a bear with three ribs gripped in its teeth; the third was like a leopard having four wings of a fowl and four heads; and the fourth beast was dreadful and exceedingly strong. It is pictured with iron teeth and ten horns.

Beginning with verse seventeen in chapter seven, the vision is interpreted for Daniel. "These great beasts, which are four, are four kings, which shall arise out of the earth." All the known world from the days of Nimrod, the founder of the Assyrian or Babylonish monarchy, down to the days of Daniel, had been in a state of agitated war. This was symbolized as a great tempestuous sea. Out of this strife a king arose to establish a kingdom.

The first king, described as a lion with eagle's wings, refers to Nebuchadnezzar and the Babylonian Empire. The lion is considered king of beasts; the eagle, king of birds; thus, the Babylonian kingdom is depicted as the first and greatest of all the earthly dominions. This was expressed in the vision of the metallic image as the golden head. The eagle's wings denote the rapidity with which Nebuchadnezzar made his conquests. Eagles are known to fly higher than other birds; thus, the great height to which the kingdom soared is described. Daniel beheld in his vision that the wings were clipped and a man's heart was given to the beast. To clip the wings would render the kingdom unfit for further flight; the conquest was checked. To be no longer lionhearted but having a man's heart, is to say that Nebuchadnezzar, the lion, was humbled to act as an ordinary man. When this powerful king reached a zenith of pride, God humbled him. He was stricken with insanity and lived like a beast in the field. After a period of seven years he was restored as a man. He became humble and pious; it is believed that he died in this state.

2 The second beast, a bear with three ribs in its teeth, presents a word picture of the Medo-Persian Kingdom. Media, a mountainous, cold, rough country, had the largest species of bear. The Medes and Persians are symbolized by a bear because of their cruel, bloodthirsty nature. The bear is an all-devouring animal and describes Medo-Persians, known for their robbers and spoilers as well as their cruelty in punishment (Jer. 51:48-56). The bear is seen raising itself up on one side. Cyrus, king of Persia, arose on the borders of Chaldea, putting his nation in a position to attack.

The three ribs clutched in the jaws of the bear symbolize the three powers, Babylonian, Median, and Persian, gripped in one great empire. As ribs support a physical body, these powers supported the Medo-Persian Empire. The bear is said to devour much flesh. Medo-Persia thrived and lived at the expense of the many nations it devoured. It is noted that the silver arms of the image seen in Daniel, chapter 2, had the bloodthirsty hands of a bear.

3. The third beast to arise out of the sea is like a leopard with four wings and four heads. This represents the third kingdom or Grecian Empire with its king, Alexander the Great. The leopard is a spotted creature, a fitting emblem of the mixture of nations, customs, and languages which constituted this empire. It is also indicative of the mixed characteristics of the king, Alexander, himself. Sometimes he was mild, sober, good—even pious. At other times he was cruel, drunken, lustful and evil. He was a great conqueror. Yet, he was conquered by his own passions.

The leopard is also noted for its swiftness. Pictured with four wings, the leopard shows the rapidity with which Alexander and the Macedonians made their conquest. The Babylonians had two wings, but the Grecian kingdom is pictured with four wings to tell that they were twice as rapid. Such rapid conquest has never been equaled in history. The fact that they were wings of a fowl rather than eagle's wings indicates they would not soar as high, as long, or as far as Babylon.

Four heads on the leopard signify four generals who received appointment as kings over each of the kingdom's four divisions. The appointments were made at the death of Alexander the Great. Because of the weakness and greed of these rulers, the kingdom dropped from the brass lap of the metallic image to the feet of iron.

4. The fourth beast presents a dreadful creature, exceedingly strong, with iron teeth and ten horns. This is a portrait of the Roman Empire crushing all nations as residue under its feet. We are acquainted with the phrase, "iron heel of Rome." It was from this dominion that the Jews of Jesus' day sought deliverance. It was different from all the other kingdoms in its republican form of government, power, extent of dominion, and length of duration. The ten horns it possessed represent the ten kingdoms into which the Roman Empire was later divided.

Attention is especially drawn to a little horn which uprooted three other horns, making room for itself. This eleventh horn had eyes of a man and a mouth speaking great things. It made war with the saints, changed times and laws, and was given dominion for time, times, and the dividing of time. After the establishment of the ten kingdoms of Rome there was another kingdom which appeared. Historical records reveal that the kingdom arising was the kingdom ruled by the pope of Rome. This horn or kingdom is said to be "more stout than his fellows" (Daniel 7:20). It is thus expressed because he possessed both religious and temporal jurisdiction while the others exerted only temporal authority. The papal kingdom grew larger and forced its power over other kingdoms. It is said that this horn had "eyes." Here is reference to the pope, who calls himself the overseer of the overseers. Even today the pope bears the title the

"Holy See." The horn also had a mouth speaking "great things," even to speaking against the Most High, changing times, laws, and seasons (Dan. 7:25). All this is fulfilled in the papacy. The pope of Rome assumes he is infallible, professes power to forgive sins, and grants indulgences for sin. This is to blaspheme God. The pope endeavors to change the time of salvation from this present world to a purgatorial hereafter. Forming his own calendar of fast or feast days, he includes the right to institute his own laws or articles of faith, making them superior to God's Holy Scripture. Indeed, the Roman Catholic church claims to possess the only set of keys to God's kingdom. While they may possess some keys, it is gratifying to know that all true Christians possess more than keys; they have the Door, Jesus Christ the Lord. Amusing, yet pathetic, was the sign on a church bulletin board which read in large bold letters, "The Gateway to Heaven." Under this caption was the announcement, "Closed for the Summer Months." No church is the gate of heaven; Jesus alone is the means of entrance.

Some interpreters believe that Peter was selected as chief custodian of the keys to the kingdom of God. Christ spoke of the keys to the kingdom on more than one occasion. After reading the familiar passage on this topic recorded in Matthew 16:19, it is well to turn to Matthew 18:18; the same commission for using the keys is given but Peter is not even mentioned. The Master's words are addressed to all the disciples. If Christ gave to Peter the sole authority for granting permission to enter the kingdom, it is strange that our Lord admitted the dying thief without even consulting Peter. Of course, we have no record that Peter was present at the crucifixion.

Realizing that the kingdom of God is a spiritual kingdom, we understand that the keys are also spiritual. The keys are labeled *prayer, new birth, repentance, obedience, love, forgiveness, and faith.*

KEYS TO THE KINGDOM

Prayer—"Thy kingdom come" Matthew 6:10.

Repentance—"Repent, the kingdom of heaven is at hand" Matthew 4:17.

Forgive—"If we forgive not . . ." Mark 11:26.

New Birth—"Except a man be born again . . ." John 3:5-7.

Love—"Greatest commandment" Matthew 22:37-40.

Obedience—"He that doeth the will of my Father . . ." Matthew 7:21.

Faith—"Believe in the Lord Jesus" Acts 16:31.

No one enters the kingdom of God without them; by the same token, every Christian possesses them to help others find their way into the kingdom. What a tremendous responsibility it is to be a custodian of these seven golden keys! They are used to loose the sinner from the prison house of sin and to open heaven's gates to eternal life. These keys have power to bind the forces of Satan and "sin shall not have dominion over you" (Rom. 6:14). Heaven had decreed that man should be redeemed from sin and receive power to overcome the world. The Scriptures declare, "For ever, O Lord, thy word is settled in heaven" (Ps. 119:89). Christ came to fulfill what had already been bound in heaven. "For this purpose the Son of God was manifested, that he might destroy the works of the devil" (1 John 3:8). Christ defines His purpose in His first sermon in Nazareth when He reads from the scroll of Isaiah saying, "The Spirit of the Lord is upon me, because he hath anointed me to preach the gospel to the poor; he hath sent me to heal the brokenhearted, to preach deliverance to the captives, and recovering of sight to the blind, to set at liberty them that are bruised" (Luke 4:18). Jesus said on another occasion, "But if I cast out devils by the Spirit of God, then the kingdom of God is come unto you" (Matt. 12:28). Please note that the casting out or binding of Satan and the coming of the kingdom of God are associated together. It was by the power of the *Word* of Christ who was anointed by the *Spirit* that souls were delivered from the bondage of sin. Christ commissioned His disciples to continue the work He had come to do saying, ". . . As my Father hath sent me, even so send I you. And when he had said this, he breathed on them, and saith unto them, Receive ye the Holy Ghost: Whose soever sins ye remit, they are remitted unto them; and whose soever sins ye retain, they are retained" (John 20:21-23). When Jesus departed to be with the Father, He sent the Holy Ghost to be the sole Administrator of the church. He also left the witness of His Word. It is by the witness of the Spirit and the Word working through Christians of today that sinners are saved; their sins are remitted. Others who refuse these witnesses of God are lost and their sins are retained. Our Lord expresses the agreement in heaven with the work of His Word and Spirit upon earth when He explains, whatsoever is bound or loosed upon earth is likewise bound or loosed in heaven. It was this thought Jesus set forth when He taught us to pray, "Thy kingdom come. Thy will be done in earth, as it is in heaven" (Matt. 6:10).

When Christians refused to accept the false claims of the Roman Catholic church, cruel persecutions broke forth. There were religious wars, crusades, massacres, and inquisitions in which millions of Christians suffered death rather than bow to the pope of Rome. Thus Daniel's prophecy was fulfilled when he foretold the rising of an eleventh horn on the Roman beast which would make war with the saints, and prevail against them (Dan. 7:21).

5. The exciting part of the vision is the establishment of God's kingdom. The kingdoms of men have been seen as one beastly nation devouring another. Thrones of earth perished and kingdoms fell. It was not to be so in the kingdom God established. "The saints of the most High shall take the kingdom, and possess the kingdom for ever, even for ever and ever" (Dan. 7:18). The vision of earthly kingdoms furnishes a background for the beautiful picture of the kingdom of God. The contrast is obvious. Kingdoms of earth are always being left to other people, but the saints eternally possess the kingdom of God. Temporal kingdoms established with a sword will perish by the sword.

God's kingdom is established in the souls of men. Jesus, Founder of the kingdom, exclaims in Pilate's judgment hall, "My kingdom is not of this world: if my kingdom were of this world, then would my servants fight, that I should not be delivered to the Jews: but now is my kingdom not from hence" (John 18:36).

The promise of victory to the saints was not to exempt them from great battle. Every generation of righteous people must face earthly foes. Likewise, every nation must come in contact with the true God. Pharaoh of Egypt met God through Moses. Babylon faced God through Daniel and the Hebrew children. Rome was destined to come into direct contact with the Son of God. It was when Rome had ascended to its political peak that Christ came to establish His kingdom. The kingdom of God is universal; while established in the days of Rome in a small country of Palestine, it is destined to fill the earth. "And this gospel of the kingdom shall be preached in all the world for a witness unto all nations; and then shall the end come" (Matt. 24:14).

Daniel's prophecy foretold of the conflict between the force of the Roman Empire and the power of the kingdom of God. Rome gloried in her military might, magnificent buildings, gold, influence and a spreading empire. Jesus proclaimed truth, love, holy ideals, meekness and faith. To the masses of people blinded with materialism, these virtues seemed trivial in comparison. Caesar could command legions around him and march in great conquests demanding nations to fall at his feet. Jesus had a small band of unlearned fishermen. Noted for His poverty, He possessed the power to compel through the great force of love. Jesus was beaten, crucified, and buried while Caesar remained upon his throne. Pit Jesus against the monarch! But Caesar, with his armies, wealth, influence, and kingdom have vanished, never to return. Jesus, a name proclaimed in every land, lives forever. The truth, love and faith He expressed abide for all eternity.

The fate of every nation is determined by accepting or rejecting Jesus and His kingdom. Judgment falls upon nations in this time world. They rise in time and must be judged in time.

We will not appear as nations at the final judgment, but as individuals. God has already judged many nations. Nations, like individuals, must reap as they sow. It makes the soul tremble to remember some sins our own nation of America must reap. Is not America's pride like that of Babylon? Does her greed equal that of MedoPersia? Will she die in a drunken stupor as Alexander the Great? Does her lust and immorality compare with Sodom? Can it be that America has joined other nations in making the world as wicked as it was in the days of Noah? We must never forget, "The wicked shall be turned into hell, and all the nations that forget God" (Ps. 9:17).

There are several key facts to be observed from the preceding symbols.

1. **Political powers** are symbolized by creatures of *animal life* (such as a lion or bear, *etc.*)

2. **Religious powers** are symbolized by characters taken from *human life.* (Example: eyes of a man; mouth speaking, *etc.*)

3. The Bible is not a crystal ball to foretell all political events. *The political powers considered are those which have a direct impact with the children of God.* (Old Testament Israelites—New Testament Christians.)

4. **Parallel themes** with varied symbols are used to present different phases of the same basic truth.

Another vital key to prophecy is the:

Key to Prophetic Time

There are a number of different calendars in existence. The most common ones in current use are the Roman (chiefly in Christendom), Chinese, Jewish and Mohammedan calendars. Each of these includes twelve months of the year but the number of days in each month varies. In the long span of prophecies, many changes have transpired in calendar dates. This creates a difficult problem in "date setting" of prophecy.

Daniel was a Jew and used the Hebrew calendar, each month having an equal number of thirty days. The measurement for prophetic time was, *"a day is equal to one year."* When the Israelites complained and murmured in the wilderness, God told Moses and Aaron that they would remain in the wilderness for forty years. God said, "After the number of the days in which ye searched the land, even forty days, *each day for a year,* shall ye bear your iniquities, even forty years" (Num. 14:34). Again, it is written in the prophecies of Ezekiel, *"I have appointed thee each day for a year"* (Ezek. 4:6b).

Daniel, the key book of symbols, gives a good example of the year-day standard of reckoning prophetic time. Daniel had been deeply concerned about the Jewish nation. When he saw visions of the rising kingdoms of earth, he was eager to know the future of his own people. Daniel was aware of Jeremiah's prophecy telling of the seventy years the Hebrew people would remain in Babylon's captivity (Jer. 25:11-12). Daniel witnessed the end of those seventy years. It was true that the Jewish people would be released from slavery in Babylon and be permitted to restore Jerusalem; however, the part of Jeremiah's prophecy which troubled Daniel was concerned with a period of seventy years. "For thus saith the Lord, That after seventy years be accomplished at Babylon I will visit you, and perform my good word toward you, in causing you to return to this place" (Jer. 29:10). The angel, Gabriel, explained to Daniel that many prophecies have a literal and a spiritual fulfillment (Dan. 9:21-27). The literal fulfillment was the release of the Jewish people at the end of seventy years' captivity. The spiritual fulfillment would be after seventy weeks of years. That would mean seventy times seven or four hundred ninety years (a day for a year) beginning with the decree of Artaxerxes to rebuild Jerusalem. The spiritual fulfillment pointed to the coming of the great Liberator, Jesus Christ, who releases souls from the bondage of sin. King Artaxerxes gave the decree in 457 B.C. Four hundred and ninety years later (A.D. 33), the ministry, death, resurrection, and ascension of Christ came to pass. Christ made claim as the Deliverer of Israel saying, "The Spirit of the Lord is upon me, because he hath anointed me to preach the gospel to the poor; he hath sent me to heal the brokenhearted, to preach deliverance to the captives, and recovering of the sight to the blind, to set at liberty them that are bruised, to preach the acceptable year of the Lord" (Luke 4:18). After reading thus from Isaiah's prophecy, Jesus uttered, "This day is this scripture fulfilled in your ears" (Luke 4:21).

Time measurement is by no means limited to the year-day method. The term "day" has varied meanings.

1. It may refer to a period of twenty-four hours, or from sunrise to sunset.

2. It may express an epoch of time, or span of life. We speak of the "Day of Creation" or "Day of Salvation," "Day of Grace," etc. Jesus said, "Abraham rejoiced to see my day: and he saw it, and was glad" (John 8:56). Peter informs us, "one day is with the Lord as a thousand years, and a thousand years as one day" (2 Pet. 3:8). There are also instances of a century being referred to as a day.

The word "time" itself is a measurement. When Daniel saw the "little horn" on the fourth beast, he said it would reign for "time and times, and the dividing of time" (Dan. 7:25). This power rising out of the Roman Empire was interpreted as being the papacy. The prophecy tells how long its world dominion would last while making war against the saints.

To determine the length of this period of time, it is necessary to know what is meant by the use of the word "time." Daniel tells the experience of Nebuchadnezzar's insanity and states that "seven times" passed over him in this condition (Dan. 4:23). From history it is learned that "seven years" is the length of Nebuchadnezzar's mental derangement. Since "seven times" equals "seven years," "one time" would equal "one year." Therefore, the length of the papacy's reign is figured as follows:

Time = 1 year = 12 months @ 30 days per month = 360 days
plural) Times = 2 years = 24 months @ 30 days per month = 720 days
(dividing of) Time = ½ year = 6 months @ 30 days per month = 180 days
3½ years 42 months   1,260 days

With the "day for a year" reckoning, this means that the papacy rule of the Roman Catholic church would hold supremacy for 1,260 years. This was fulfilled during the period of the "Dark Ages." The Roman church ruled the world in civil and religious matters. War was made with God's true children who suffered great persecution and death. The supremacy of Rome's authority was broken with the ushering in of the sixteenth-century Reformation.

With the foregoing set of keys to the symbols, many mysteries shall be unlocked. These serve as a basic set of rules for interpretation. There are some exceptions to the rules, but even these may be understood by the light diffused in clearly interpreted passages.

Like Daniel, author of our key book to the Revelation, we too live in perilous times. The threat of atomic war creates the fear that all civilization will be utterly destroyed. Glorious is our faith that no powers of men or demons can destroy the kingdom of God. It is written, "Wherefore we receiving a kingdom which cannot be moved, let us have grace, whereby we may serve God acceptably with reverence and godly fear" (Heb. 12:28). John describes the triumphant victory of the kingdom, saying, "And the seventh angel sounded; and there were great voices in heaven, saying, The kingdoms of this world are become the kingdoms of our Lord, and of his Christ; and he shall reign for ever and ever" (Rev. 11:15). Paul acclaims ultimate victory for the Conqueror, Christ our King, with these words: "Then cometh the end, when he shall have delivered up the kingdom to God, even the Father" (1 Cor. 15:24).

When the sun, which has shown its light from the beginning, has burned to only a cinder; the moon, which ruled the night, fades and gives light no more; tall stately trees that stood as sentinels of the centuries have fallen never to rise; the rivers, seas, and oceans cease to be; and time itself is past and gone; saints of all ages shall continue the praises to the King in the everlasting kingdom of God! Amen.

CHAPTER III

PANORAMA OF THE BEASTS

There is an old story of four blind men describing an elephant. Using his sensitive fingers for eyes, feeling the elephant's tough-skinned leg, the first blind man said, "An elephant is just like the trunk of a tree." A second sightless man twisted its tail and declared, "An elephant is like a rope." The third man pressed his hands over the massive side of the elephant and exclaimed, "An elephant is like the side of a barn." The fourth companion objected strenuously, arguing "the elephant is like a fountain." He had just been thoroughly sprayed with water from the elephant's trunk.

The spiritually blind man can never properly interpret the beasts of the Apocalypse. The eyes of the soul must be opened by the Christ who touched Bartimaeus. It is also imperative to view the entire panorama of the beasts in John's vision in order to comprehend the meaning conveyed in this strange language. Any small section isolated from the picture as a whole will lead to a distorted interpretation.

Isaiah had a vision of various beasts feeding together. He prophesied, "The wolf also shall dwell with the lamb, and the leopard shall lie down with the kid; and the calf and the young lion and the fatling together; and a little child shall lead them. And the cow and the bear shall feed; their young ones shall lie down together: and the lion shall eat straw like the ox. And the suckling child shall play on the hole of the asp, and the weaned child shall put his hand on the cockatrice' den" (Isa. 11:6-8). This animal parade on God's holy mountain is figurative speech describing the sinful, beastly natures of people being changed, making them all meek as lambs. Christ fulfilled this prophecy at His first coming. He did not die to change the animals of the field but to create a new nature in sinful men. Through the power of the cross, Christ changed the leopard's spots of sin to the innocence of a lamb. A small lad was once asked if there were a den in his house. "Oh, no," he replied, "my daddy doesn't need a den; he just roars all over the house." Christ can change the lion's temper. He came to remove the venom from human tongues that would poison the influence of others. How beautiful that we all may become sheep of the Great Shepherd and be fed in His green pastures!

Animal pictures are not limited in describing only the individual. In ancient and modern history animals are used to represent teams, groups, parties, and nations. Athletic teams are often identified as "Tigers," "Bearcats," "Lions" etc. Political and religious powers are also designated with varied symbols. England glories in the royal standard with the six golden lions on a red field. America takes pride in her golden eagle. No one questions the elephant and donkey parade near election time. The author of the Apocalypse employs this type of figurative speech in presenting the prophecies of the church.

The Star-Crowned Woman and the Great Red Dragon
(Rev. 12)
(See Picture Chart following page 32: Strip 3)

The stars were brightly shining in the unclouded canopy of the heavens over the Isle of Patmos. Shimmering rays of light from the moon above beamed upon the silvery waters of the Aegean Sea. Silence reigned everywhere. Thus, it must have been as John, the apostle, received this exquisite vision. Angels pulled the curtains of darkness back and pinned them with a star. God used the heavens as a scroll to convey to John the message for the church.

John is intrigued with the splendor of a beautiful woman appearing in the heavens. She is clothed with the sun, stands on the moon, and wears a glittering crown of twelve stars. The woman is pregnant with child and travails in birth to be delivered. John is horror stricken when he observes a great red dragon come into view on the heavenly scroll. This hideous monster appears with seven heads, ten horns, and seven crowns upon his heads. His lengthy tail draws a third part of the stars and casts them to earth. The beastly dragon stands before the woman ready to devour her child as soon as it is born. John beholds the woman give birth to a man-child who shall rule all nations with a rod of iron. Then the man-child is caught up to the throne of God and the woman flees into the wilderness where God has prepared a place for her. Here she will be fed for "One thousand two hundred and three score days."

The most beautiful part of John's vision is the star-crowned sun-clothed woman standing upon the moon. Every luminary of heaven is used to describe her glory. The key to the symbol reminds us that objects drawn from human life depict religious characters. The "woman" appearing in the heavens clothed with vestments of light symbolizes a heaven-born religion of great illumination. To John there is only one religious body worthy of such description—it is the Holy Mother Church of the New Testament! Paul presents the portrait of the church as a mother when he writes to the Galatians, saying, "Jerusalem which is above is free, which is the mother of us all" (Gal. 4:26).

This blessed mother is adorned with a diadem of twelve stars which are the twelve apostles of the Lamb. The moon on which she stands is the Old Testament light, the shadow of good things to come. The law and prophets were given to govern the night before Christ came. With the dawning of the gospel day, the Light of the World clothes His church with the Sun of righteousness (Mal. 4:2). The "moon" is not taken away. Christ did not come to destroy the law or the prophets, but to fulfill them (Matt. 5:17). The woman's standing above the moon indicates that the New Testament church is on a more elevated plane, vested with a much more brilliant Light (2 Cor. 4:4). As the natural sun gives life, warmth and healing to the earth, so Christ is all in all to His church.

This "woman," the church, is pictured as being ready to deliver a child. Centuries before John's day Isaiah saw this Holy Mother Church. He said, "Before she travailed, she brought forth; before her pain came, she was delivered of a man-child. Who hath heard such a thing? Who hath seen such things? Shall the earth be made to bring forth in one day? Or shall a *nation* be born at once? For as soon as Zion travailed, she brought forth her children" (Isa. 66:7-8).

The Psalmist has also written, "And of Zion it shall be said, This and that man was born in her" (Ps. 87:5a). Here is a description of the primitive church bringing to birth a nation of Christians who compose one body in Christ (Eph. 2:15). Isaiah's prophecy was fulfilled when the church assembled in the upper room at Jerusalem. On the day of Pentecost a new nation, three thousand souls, came to birth. As a child is of the mother—of the same flesh, blood, and nature—likewise, this symbol expresses that the church produced more of herself.

The ugly part of the vision is a horrid great red dragon. It has seven heads and ten horns, and seven crowns upon its heads. If there were such a creature, it would be in the animal kingdom; therefore, we look for some political figure to fit this description. The political power existing at the time of the establishment of the New Testament church was Pagan Rome. Looking for a dragon in the Bible we find Pharaoh of Egypt is called a dragon when he tried to kill the infant nation of Israel. "Thus saith the Lord God; Behold, I am against thee, Pharaoh king of Egypt, against the great dragon that lieth in the midst of his rivers, which has said, "My river is my own, and I have made it for myself" (Ezekiel 29:3). Nebuchadrezzar, king of Babylon is also likened to a dragon. Jeremiah writes, ". . . [Nebuchadrezzar] hath devoured me, he hath made me an empty vessel, he hath swallowed me up like a dragon, he hath filled his belly with my delicates, he hath cast me out" (Jeremiah 51:34). John, the revelator, chooses this background to reveal Pagan Rome as the dragon endeavoring to kill the infant church as soon as it was born. The "dragon" was the accepted standard, emblem, or insignia of the Roman Empire. The seven heads of the dragon signify seven forms of government which ruled consecutively as heads of the Roman kingdom. The five which had already fallen in John's day were the Regal power, the Consular, the Decemvirate, the Military Tribunes and the Imperial. To identify the ten horns we find the ten kingdoms which arose later in Rome's history. The fact that the crowns are seen on the heads rather than on the horns signifies that the sovereign rule had not yet been transferred to the ten kingdoms. This heathen power controlled by Satan was determined to destroy the newborn church. The pagan emperor demanded worship which Christians refused to give. Because they failed to burn incense on pagan altars, Christians were despised, hated and persecuted. Any disaster in the empire was blamed on the Christians. If the crops failed, Christians must be censured because they had made the gods of the Roman pantheon angry by failing to worship them. The emperor was a dictator claiming supreme allegiance to himself and the Roman state.

John saw the "tail" of this dragon cast stars to the earth. The "tail" expresses that it was the end part of the empire. The stars which fell were the gospel lights, God's ministers. Had not Rome crucified Peter? Was it not Rome's sword that severed the noble head of Paul from his shoulders? Did not Antipas and numbers of unnamed ministers suffer martyrdom? Not only putting ministers of the church to death, but devouring Christians as soon as they were born tells of masses who died in the cruel clutches of the bloodthirsty red dragon. Some were thrown to wild beasts, some stoned, others were beaten, some were burned.

It was in the year A.D. 67 while Nero, sixth emperor of Rome, was in power, that the first great persecution of the church broke forth. Nero, in the first years of his reign, ruled with credit to himself. In later years he was noted for an extravagant temper and atrocious barbarities. Eager for excitement, he ordered the city of Rome to be set on fire. His officers, guards and servants carried out the command. Nero went to the tower of

Macaenas, played his harp and sang of the burning of Troy while the imperial city was in flames. Thousands perished in the fire or were buried beneath debris. After nine days of burning, the city lay in ruins. It was noised among the people that Nero had ordered the fire; it also was heard that he wished the ruin of all things before his death.

Realizing that great hostility was expressed toward him, Nero determined to charge the Christians with this diabolical deed. The lie sentenced Christians to be put to death. Nero gloated in seeing human blood spilled in the arena of wild beasts. He even refined upon cruelty by demanding Christians, with arms tied behind their backs, to be placed in waxen shirts. They were then fastened to axletrees in Nero's gardens. Their hair was used as a wick and they were burned alive, as human torches, to illuminate the gardens of the fiendish emperor! No wonder John described Rome as a great red dragon. This is only one of the multiple ways in which Christians were persecuted.

God took note as His saints were being slain. To die in the flesh was to release the spirit or soul to ascend to God. This body of Christian martyrs is symbolized as the man-child being caught up to heaven. John had seen these souls under the altar of God at the opening of the fifth seal. The "iron-rod" which the man-child was to rule refers to the Word of God which cannot be broken. John beheld the great battle of the church in its struggle against heathen Rome as a war in the heavens. He saw the Spirit of Christ strengthening the saints in the conflict against spiritual and civil wickedness, as Michael, guardian angel of the Jewish people, had protected them in literal warfare. The battle against heathenism raged. But righteousness is greater than iniquity; truth is stronger than error; Christianity is more powerful than paganism. In spite of all the persecution and death of many saints, the number of Christians increased. Even in Paul's day many heathen temples were abandoned.

John rejoices as the vision pictures the triumph of the church and the dragon of heathenism cast down. We thrill with the beloved Apostle as we hear the glad shout, "And the great dragon was cast out, that old serpent, called the Devil, and Satan, which deceiveth the whole world: he was cast out into the earth, and his angels were cast out with him" (Rev. 12:9). With the dawning of truth in the morning of the gospel day, the darkness of pagan error was destined to fade. With the victory of the church came the triumphant cry, "And I heard a loud voice saying in heaven, Now is come salvation, and strength, and the kingdom of our God, and the power of his Christ: for the accuser of our brethren is cast down, which accused them before our God day and night" (Rev. 12:10). It is easily understood that the battle was a spiritual conflict because the saints overcame the power of Satan "by the blood of the Lamb, and by the word of their testimony; and they loved not their lives unto the death" (Rev. 12:11).

At this point in history, Constantine, the first Christian emperor, ascended the imperial throne. When Constantine was entering Italy in his conquest to conquer the world, it is said he saw a vision of a flaming cross in the sky. According to historians, there was an inscription under the cross which Constantine interpreted, "By this sign conquer." After his coronation in A.D. 323 Constantine professed Christianity himself and made Christianity the official religion of the Roman State. The victory was symbolized with a large picture of Constantine erected over the palace gate. There was a cross over the emperor's head, and under his feet was the form of a dragon transfixed with a dart through the middle of its body, and falling headlong into the sea.[1]

When pagan Rome saw its prestige was lost and its political power crushed at the time Constantine became emperor, it sought new means to destroy the church. The true church is seen as a woman fleeing from a beast. God's saints were driven into seclusion but God had prepared a place of safety where she was

---

[1]Smith, F. G., *Revelation Explained*, p. 164.

nurtured for One thousand, two hundred and three score days, or as it is written, "For time, times, and half of time." This equals 1,260 years in prophetic time.

The church had no more than conquered paganism until it was faced with a new conflict. Fleeing into the wilderness expresses that the true church would be hidden while a false religion would rule the world. The eagle's wings depict strength for a safe flight (Exod. 19:4). Here is an allusion to the Old Testament story of Elijah. While famine prevailed and prophets of Baal seduced Israel into idolatry, Elijah, God's prophet, was secretly fed and nourished in the wilderness for three years and six months (1 Kings 17, 18). This equals twelve hundred and sixty years in prophetic time.[2]

Sad grew the soul of John to see the holy church flee into hiding while a false church led the world into idolatry and spiritual famine prevailed. Then, faith, courage, and hope inspired the revelator's heart as assurance came that the church could never be destroyed. Though the prophecies told that the church would be secluded, oppressed and persecuted for a long period of time, she would triumph again. The same power which gave victory over Pagan Rome would preserve and keep the church, then lead again to victory for the saints. How true are the words of our Christ, ". . . I will build my church; and the gates of hell shall not prevail against it" (Matt. 16: 18b).

The Leopard Beast (Rev. 13:1-10)

Readers today are left to wonder concerning minor details of John's revelation received near the end of the first century. We may aptly suppose that the vision of a weird beast came after the night had passed. The God who used the heavens as a scroll now chooses to use the sea as a canvas. The heavenly scroll, embossed with a star-crowned woman and a great red dragon, vanishes from view with the rising of the morning sun.

---

[2]See Time Table, p. 58.

Ascending out of the sea is a monstrous wild beast, having seven heads, and ten crowned horns. It is spotted like a leopard, has feet like a bear, and a mouth like a lion. This beast also has human characteristics and is capable of worship, speaking and making war. These symbols drawn from both animal and human life point to a political-religious body.

Historical records establish the fact that when the old pagan Roman Empire fell a new Papal Rome took form as the papacy increased in power. Papal Rome is governed by the pope of the Roman Catholic church which believes in the combination of church and state. With this set of symbols we will see the Roman Catholic church in the light of prophecy.

A "beast" in prophecy delineates a political power. A "wild beast" depicts a tyrannical empire. John said this "beast" received its power, seat, and authority from the dragon (paganism). Satan simply changed his pagan garb and appears in the vestments of popery.

As soon as Constantine made Christianity the official state religion, everyone was forced to take this form of religious faith. Numbers of pagans were never converted—they simply adopted Christian customs. Many Christians relaxed in their Christian endeavor and witness; thus, Rome protracted into its new form many laws, systems, customs, and practices from the ancient empire.

The "beast" is described with seven heads and ten horns. Each time Rome is pictured as the beast in prophecy, it appears with all the heads and horns it ever had. These seven heads wore the crowns of sovereignty when Rome was pictured in its pagan form as the dragon. Under the new empire symbol, the crowns of sovereignty are transferred to the ten kingdoms of Rome, symbolized as horns. These ten Roman kingdoms are as follows:

1. Anglo-Saxons	6. Lombards
2. Bergundians	7. Ostrogoths
3. Franks	8. Suevi
4. Huns	9. Vandals
5. Heruli	10. Visigoths

It is interesting to observe that these are the same kingdoms Daniel saw in his vision of the fourth beast with ten horns. Daniel also saw another kingdom rise to uproot these Kingdoms, making room for its supremacy. The fulfillment came in the rising of the papacy which usurped rule over all other kingdoms and made the pope the supreme authority of all religious and temporal matters.

Ancient Rome was governed by a college of priests. A high priest, addressed as Pontifix Maximus, was elected from within the college. He exerted supreme authority in religious law, marriage, and social matters. Emperor Augustus combined this office of high priest with his position as emperor; thus, his dictates became supreme in all civil and religious matters. Succeeding emperors down to Gratian in A.D. 382 continued this practice. Following the same pattern, the papacy established a high priest in Rome. He was later called a pope which really means "papa" or "father." Gradually, the pope's authority increased. He was regarded as supreme head of the church, exerted civil and religious power, and even carried over the title, "Pontifix Maximus." To this day he is clothed officially in the same attire as the ancient pagan high priest. He is more commonly known as the "Pontiff."

Pagan Rome worshipped the goddess Vesta, one of the twelve Roman deities. She was regarded as the goddess of the hearth and home. In the temple of Vesta, built in the Forum at Rome, there was no image or statue, but an eternal fire was her symbol and it must be kept burning continually. Little girls between the ages of six and ten years were given by their parents to be servants in the temple of Vesta. Sometimes the Pontifix Maximus chose these Vestal Virgins himself. They spent thirty years as priestesses in the temple. If they ever broke their vows they were to be buried alive. The Catholic nuns have copied their religious order from this pagan worship. It may be noted that the orders of monks and altar boys also have their origin in antiquity.

Another example of dragon worship being perpetuated is the wearing of medals, scapulars, images, and charms. This originated with the heathen, but is promoted in the Roman Catholic church as a means of protection. The process of deification has changed in name to canonization. The pagans burned incense and worshipped their great men as gods after their death. Roman Catholics canonize saints, offer prayers, and set special days of homage to the departed souls of the righteous. Papalism is the worship of the pope, Virgin Mary, and the saints.

In the year A.D. 610, Pope Boniface IV took possession of the Roman Pantheon.[3] This circular building had been constructed in the year A.D. 27 by Marcus Agrippa for the purpose of unifying the empire. It was dedicated to all the Roman and Greek gods. Here were idols of Jupiter, father of the gods; Apollo, the sun god; Diana, virgin goddess of the moon; Mars, god of war; Venus, goddess of love; and numerous other images. Pope Boniface changed the inscription over the door, which was "To All the Gods," to read, "To the Blessed Virgin and All the Saints." The names of the idols were changed to designate the various saints. Roman Catholics entered the same building, worshipped the same idols, and sometimes uttered the same prayers as the pagans had before them. In this way the beast worshipped the dragon.

These instances express how Papal Rome was a mixture of truth and error. It was part good and part bad—it it was both dark and light. Rome, spotted with the light of Christianity over the dark spread of pagan idolatry, appears as a spotted leopard. It wore a cloak called "Christian Rome," but it was pagan in heart —only Christian in name.

The true church had wielded a dreadful blow against one of the heads of Pagan Rome. It almost wounded paganism to death; but when persecution ceased, Christians became complacent. The deadly wound was healed and all the world wandered after Papal Rome. The increasing power of the pope became very dangerous. He demanded supreme allegiance. His laws were to be

---

[3]*Grolier Encyclopedia*, Vol.8, p. 206.

strictly enforced. Anyone failing to recognize the pope as the infallible head of the church was pronounced a heretic. Heretics were sentenced to death. Again, persecution fires were set aflame. The atrocious murders of Pagan Rome did not even compare with the horrors of papal massacres. Under the guise of Christianity, Papal Rome, as a bloodthirsty bear, trampled the bodies of true saints under her feet by the millions.

Refusing to bow to the error, superstition, and idolatry demanded by the Catholic pope, multitudes were imprisoned, starved, beaten, devoured by wild beasts and burned alive! Dominic, a monk, very zealous for the cause of popery, instituted an order named, "Dominican Friars." They proceeded against whomever they pleased with no consideration of age, sex, or rank. This order confiscated homes and property of anyone labeled "heretic." The order is still a strong hand of Catholicism and operates in most countries of the world, including America.

These horrid persecutions forced many true saints to the catacombs and wilderness places. Some felt strength in banding together. Learning there was a strong group of so-called heretics in Paris, France, it was planned to destroy them all in one blow. By the command of the Catholic church, soldiers burst into the city at a given signal and a slaughter began in every direction. An admiral was killed and thrown out a window into the street, where his head was cut off and sent to the pope. The savage papists cut off his arms and private members, and after dragging him three days through the streets, hanged him up by his heels outside the city. In the first three days of the massacre they slew to the number of ten thousand. The bodies were thrown into the rivers; blood ran with a current through the streets. This was called "Saint Bartholomew's Massacre" and transpired in August, A.D. 1572. From Paris, destruction spread throughout the empire.[4]

The cruelty of this "beast," Papal Rome, was further expressed in the murder of infants and children. In order to cause

---

[4]*Fox's Book of Martyrs*, p. 47.

parents to relinquish their Christian faith, small babies were taken to the arena of the wild beasts. They were tied in animal skins and attached to a long pole. In the presence of the parents the child was let down by inches into the arena. Amid the screams of the innocent, authorities demanded parents to recant. Often mothers fainted and suffered the same fate as their children. In all such persecutions, the "beast" of papalism made war with the saints.

Both Daniel and John described the mouth of the beast. Daniel said the beast would "speak great words against the most High" (Dan. 7:25). John said it was "as the mouth of a lion." Also he spoke "great things and blasphemies." The blasphemies were "against God, to blaspheme his name, and his tabernacle, and them that dwell in heaven" (Rev. 13:5-6). The pope of Rome blasphemes God by claiming God's authority. Only God can forgive sin. The Holy Father in heaven alone is infallible. There is but one head of the church—Jesus Christ. The pope speaks blasphemy against God's name by claiming such titles as "Holy Father," "Lord God the Pope," "Vicar of the Son of God," and others. Popery is guilty of blaspheming the saints, those who dwell in heaven, by veneration and the offering of prayers through them.

This mouth of blasphemy ascribed to Papal Rome utters its own laws, and with the roar of a lion demands that they be obeyed. It boasts of its power and dares the world to oppose its position. It is noted that "all that dwell upon the earth shall worship him, whose names are not written in the book of life of the Lamb" (Rev. 13:8). But the supremacy was not to remain forever. The time allotted by the prophecy was forty-two months.[5] This is equal to the 1,260 years the church was hidden in the wilderness. This promise meant much to the Christians of the Dark Ages. They knew the day would come when the Roman Catholic church could no longer rule the world. While she lost her

---

[5]See Time Table on p. 58.

supremacy with the breaking forth of Protestantism, it is destined that the Roman beast (Catholicism) will remain until the end of time as an enemy of true Christianity.

Paul said, "And then shall that Wicked be revealed, whom the Lord shall consume with the spirit of his mouth, and shall destroy with the brightness of his coming" (2 Thess. 2:8).

The Lamblike Beast (Rev. 13:11-18)

God, the great Artist, paints with the luminaries of the heavens, and draws His sketches on the canvas of the sea; then He chooses to make the earth as a parchment to unfold great truth.

Again, a dual symbol of beastly characteristics and human attributes is combined in the creature of John's vision. Coming up out of the earth is a beastlike lamb with two horns. It speaks like the dragon and exercises authority as the leopard beast. Here is another combination of political and religious authority expressed as church and state. Chronologically, the religious body appearing at the end of Roman Catholic supremacy is **Protestantism.** Being as a **lamb** indicates that this political-religious system is much more docile than the Roman Catholic power described as a **leopard** beast. It has already been explained that "horn" denotes power. The two horns of this lamblike beast describe the two great powers of primitive Protestantism, church and state.

Martin Luther, an Augustinian monk of Germany, became deeply concerned with religious conditions in the Catholic church. While studying as a monk, he accidentally found a Latin Bible. Having never seen one before he read it with intense interest. Luther was amazed to learn that such a small part of the Scriptures was taught to the people. He was especially intrigued with the Epistle to the Romans. The text, "Being justified freely by his grace through the redemption that is in Christ Jesus: Whom God hath set forth to be a propitiation through faith in his blood, to declare his righteousness for the remission of sins that are past . . ." (Rom. 3:24-25), became a beacon light of truth. Teaching salvation by faith was contrary to Catholic dogma of redemption by works. In addition to disputing a number of Catholic articles of faith, Luther sternly contradicted the sale of indulgences.

Upon the eve of All Saints Day, AD. 1517, Martin Luther publicly posted a thesis opposing the sale of indulgences. Immediately thereafter, Tetzel, a Dominican friar, came selling indulgences in the streets. He shouted, "I save more souls with these indulgences than Peter saved with his sermons." Tetzel also made claims of deliverance granted to souls in purgatory as soon as their loved ones in this world paid sufficient funds for their indulgences. The sale of indulgences was promoted by the Catholic pope to secure money for the building of Saint Peter's Cathedral in Rome. To increase sales, indulgences were sold, not only for committed sins of the past, but to cover future sins. It is quite shocking to learn that the sale of indulgences continues to this day. One of the largest sources of revenue in the Catholic church is money from masses offered in behalf of souls in purgatory. Great sums also are received when money is paid as penalty fines by multitudes who do penances. High money means high mass; low money means low mass; no money means no mass.

The sale of indulgences was as a fuse to set afire great protest against Catholicism. Because of this protest, Luther and his many followers were named Protestants. This was a great day for the church—the Reformation was rising to action. Martin Luther translated the Bible into the German language. This was powerful ammunition for truth! Following great confusion and stern opposition, a climax was reached when the first Protestant creed was adopted in A.D. 1530. Protestantism grew rapidly in Germany. Even the pope was terrified at the success of Luther, the courageous reformer. Religious war broke out; thousands died in the conflict. Due to these persecutions numbers of Protestants fled into England during the reign of Queen Anne. Here they were cordially received and given humane assistance as well as financial aid. While it is true that the roots of Protestantism spread into France, Spain, Switzerland, the Netherlands and others, the greatest strongholds for Protestantism were Germany and England.

Protestantism became a state religion. Just as Luther gave a state church to Germany, King Henry VIII gave a state church to England. This religion of Protestantism was forced upon all citizens of the state. Protestants were guilty of persecuting and killing Catholics as well as Anabaptists and other religious groups who differed with Protestant laws; thus, the lamblike beast speaks like the dragon. It was Protestant persecution that forced Puritans and Pilgrims to American shores for religious freedom. It must be noted that Protestantism made an

Image of the Beast

The likeness between the beast (Catholicism) and the image of the beast (Protestantism) is conspicuous. Both have exerted authority in religious and political matters. They each claim power and right to admit or excommunicate individuals as church members; priest and preacher claim such authority. The Catholic church has made her own canonical laws to govern this religious body; Protestantism has formed her own creeds, disciplines and manuals. Such names as "Saint Mary's Church," "Saint Joseph's Church," etc. appear on Catholic edifices. Protestants also name their assemblies "Saint Luke's," "Saint John's," "Lutherans," "Wesleyans," "Baptists," and numerous others. Dogma of Catholic faith proclaims a purgatory as a future opportunity for salvation after death. This is reflected in the Millennial belief of some Protestants; both offer salvation after death. It has long been stated as absurd for one body to have two heads. The Catholics claim the pope as earthly head of the church, and Christ as the heavenly head. Protestants, however, have numerous bodies all claiming one head. Which is the greater monstrosity?

The Mark of the Beast

How blessed to know that Protestant bodies have broken free from the bondage of Catholicism. Praises be to God for great reformers of the Reformation! The picture becomes deplorable, however, when marks of Catholicism become so evident in Protestant churches. Ecclesiastical rule and human government in divine matters bear an imitation of the hierarchy of Rome. The manner of church membership in Protestantism is a marked carry-over of the Catholic system. Names on church membership rolls include numbers of persons who have joined church as a matter of form and experienced no spiritual rebirth. The New Testament teaches that members are added to the Body of Christ by a new birth. The mode of sprinkling for baptism is a definite imprint of Roman Catholic faith. Many forms, rituals, traditions, and customs of Protestantism have Catholic origin. Many bodies of Protestant faith are uniting under one head. This union plan may sound like the real Lamb of God calling all sheep to one fold. Remember, John saw a lamb in his vision which spake as a dragon; it also had marks of the first beast. Is it not true that there is only one Head over the church in heaven and earth, the Lord Jesus Christ? It is written, ". . . Christ is the head of the church: and he is the saviour of the body" (Eph. 5:23).

Perhaps one of the most dangerous marks of Catholicism imbedded in Protestant religions is the deception of multitudes. Millions believe they are saved because they are Catholics and the priest has by formal rites admitted them into the church. Many also believe they are saved because of a formal membership and adherence to articles of belief in Protestant doctrine. Most of the great number of lost souls are those who had religion but not salvation. The Holy Scriptures plainly express the requirement for eternal life. "He that hath the Son hath life; and he that hath not the Son of God hath not life" (1 John 5:12).

It is said by John that the lamblike beast imposed the mark of the beast upon "both small and great, rich and poor, free and bond" (Rev. 13:16). The mark was in their foreheads or in their right hand. This is figurative speech expressing ownership. As a slave was marked in his forehead, so all would know to whom he belonged, in like manner, every person reveals his brand of religion with the religious name and deeds he bears. When John speaks of the mark in the right hand, it indicates the giving of a hand of fellowship to persons who adhere to certain requirements for membership. No one could buy or sell save he had the mark, name or number of the beast. Buying and selling is a means of exchange. This, no doubt, has a spiritual application indicating that persons who refuse to accept the marks of Catholicism already described in this chapter, sever their ties of fellowship and have no dealings with the religious bodies which demand them. For example, in most religious sects it is required that one join the church, accept all its doctrine and adhere to its creeds or discipline. Failure to do so excommunicates the individual from the privileges and benefits of the religious body.

While it is agreed that there is a spiritual application of receiving marks of the beast, there is also a further consideration of the matter. The beast (Roman Catholic church) imposes its name and mark upon all within its reach. Particularly in Catholic-controlled countries is force used to pressure non-Catholics into the Catholic mold. No names of non-Catholics ever appear on a political ballot—only Catholics are permitted to public office. Business establishments owned or operated by non-Catholics are often boycotted.

Reverend C. Stanley Lowell, associate director of Protestants and Other Americans United for Separation of Church and State, relates the following information in the article "A Summons to Americans." Using Spain for an example of a Catholic-controlled country he points out these facts: "Protestant marriages and funeral services are forbidden in Spain. A Protestant cannot send his children to school unless he consents to having Roman Catholic teaching forced on them. Two young men of the navy, members of the Assembly of the Brethren in Vigo, Spain, received sentence of two years in prison for refusing to genuflect at a Roman Catholic Mass which navy law had required them to attend. The higher Court of Justice reaffirmed their sentence and advised them that repetition of their "crime" would bring repetition of the sentence. Favoritism is expressed in hiring employees for any kind of public labor; Catholics always have preference over non-Catholics; thus, there is a religious, social, political, and economical pressure used to force individuals into the Catholic mold. It is astounding to note the measure of pressure already used in America by Catholics endeavoring to imprint marks of the beast upon all Americans. The Bible is filled with contrasts: Good, Bad, Right, Wrong, Truth and Error, and many others. The Revelation makes a contrast with the symbols of Beast and Lamb. Satan is a beast from the beginning. He appears as a serpent, a lion, a bear, a leopard, dragon and other symbols. Jesus is spoken of as the Lamb of God numerous times. Jesus has placed a seal of protection on all of His followers. It is written, "The foundation of God standeth sure, having this seal, the Lord knoweth them that are his. And, Let everyone that nameth the name of Christ depart from iniquity" (II Timothy 2:19). Followers of the Lamb are marked with His blood, they carry a cross, they portray His image, they are sealed with His Spirit (". . . after that ye believed, ye were sealed with the holy Spirit of promise" Ephesians 1:13b). Christians are also marked with the Father's Name in our foreheads (Rev. 14:1), the symbol of ownership.

Satan also makes marks as a beast. His followers are marked with iniquity. They are bound with chains of sin's bondage. They bear the likeness of Satan's image. Satan's spirit is expressed in their lives. To some unbelieving Jews, Jesus said, "Ye are of your father, the devil, and the lusts of your father you will do. He was a murderer from the beginning, and abode not in the truth" (John 8:44).

Everyone is marked. We are identified with the Lamb of God, or we are marked by the beast, Satan. Souls have been marked since time began.

Next to claim attention is:

The Number of the Beast

John wrote, "Here is wisdom. Let him that hath understanding count the number of the beast: for it is the number of a man; and his number is Six hundred threescore and six" (Rev. 13:18). It has already been established that the "beast" refers to the Roman Catholic church. The most prominent man in the papacy is the pope. His official title used especially on the day that he is crowned as supreme head of the church is "Vicarius Filii Dei"—which means Vicar of the Son of God. The Roman letters IVXLCDM possess numerical value. The letters "U" and "V" are used interchangeably and equal the same value of five. To learn the number of the pope, the letters of his title appear as follows:

V-5	F-0
I-1	I-1
C-100	L-50
A-0	I-1
R-0	I-1
I-1	D-500
U-5	E-0
S-0	<u>I-1</u>
Vicarius Filii Dei	666

It is not by coincidence that the word Lateinos, which means "the Latin kingdom," contains the number 666. The Hebrew name for the Roman beast which is "Romuth" also verifies the number 666. Here is the testimony in Roman, Hebrew, and Latin.[6] The footnotes in my Catholic Bible interpret this figure to represent Caesar Nero. This really establishes the close relationship between Pagan and Papal Rome. The papa's (pope's) name numbers the same as the grandpapa's (Caesar's).

---

[6]Adam Clarke's *Commentary,* p. 1026.

The Lamb on Mount Zion (Rev. 14)

Mountain peaks have often been used as a scaffold, lifting high many glorious experiences between God and man. On Mount Moriah God met with Abraham. At Mount Sinai God gave the law to Moses. Mount Carmel was the scene of God's power sending fire to consume Elijah's sacrifice. On Mount Hermon Jesus was transfigured, and from Mount Olivet He ascended. There are numbers of other mountain-top experiences. The last to be mentioned in the Scriptures is John's vision of Mount Zion. On the highest elevation of the Isle of Patmos, God paints the symbol of a lamb and one hundred forty-four thousand worshippers, with the Father's name in their foreheads.

The lamb is not an ordinary animal; as such, it would refer to a political power. It is the sacrificial Lamb of God. When Abraham took Isaac to Mount Moriah, Isaac inquired concerning the sacrifice. Abraham said, "God will provide himself a lamb" (Gen. 22:8a). The literal fulfillment was that a sacrifice was found in the thicket and offered instead of Isaac. The spiritual fulfillment was Jesus, God's only Son, offered as a sacrifice for the world. He is the Lamb that God provided which was slain from the foundation of the world (Rev. 13:8b). This lamb on Mount Zion is the same one John saw being worshipped before the throne of God (Rev. 5:6). John the Baptist also declared Jesus to be "the Lamb of God, which taketh away the sin of the world" (John 1:29). The law of symbols forbids changing the character of the object portrayed. The lamb cannot be a symbol of a symbol, therefore it continues to represent the Body of Christ in its redemptive capacity.

The true Lamb makes a striking contrast with the monstrous beasts in the great parade of the centuries. We thrill with the soul of John to see the real Body of Christ in full view near the end of time. John had seen the vision of the church fleeing into the wilderness, while the beast of Catholicism raged and paraded like a roaring lion. He also witnessed in the vision the second stage of apostasy, as the two-horned lamb of Protestantism emerged and wandered in great confusion. Then God depicts his true church, whole and complete again on Mount Zion.

The term "Zion" must be interpreted. Literally, it is the highest peak in Jerusalem and sometimes refers to all Jerusalem as a city. The terms "Zion" and "Jerusalem" are used interchangeably. This is the primitive church of the early morning era. She was seen going into the wilderness and hidden during the Dark Ages. Now in the evening time of the gospel day this holy Zion is pictured again in great beauty. Paul also used the metaphor of the holy city to portray the church saying, "But ye are come unto Mount Zion, and unto the city of the living God, the heavenly Jerusalem, and to an innumerable company of angels, to the general assembly and church of the firstborn, which are written in heaven, and to God the Judge of all, and to the spirits of just men made perfect, and to Jesus the mediator of the new covenant" (Heb. 12:22-24).

To the Jew, Jerusalem meant the habitation of Jehovah. He believed that God's dwelling was in the Holy of Holies of the temple. This temple also was where the high priest offered the sacrifice for sins and atonement. To the Christian, Jerusalem means the true church, God's habitation through the Spirit. It is where Christ, our High Priest, has made the sacrifice of His own blood for our atonement. Seeing Mount Zion as the great mountain of truth at the end of time establishes the prophecy of the Psalmist saying, "They that trust in the Lord shall be as Mount Zion, which cannot be removed, but abideth for ever" (Ps. 125:1).

Next to claim attention are the 144,000 worshippers. In chapter seven of the Revelation, John identifies this host of worshippers as the true Israel of God. Literal Israel was only a figure or type of spiritual Israel—the church. Comparisons between the two are many. Physical Jews were such by birth, circumcision, and obedience to the law of Moses. One becomes a spiritual Jew by the new birth, circumcision of the heart, and obedience to the law of Christ. Paul explains it thus: "For he is not a Jew, which is one outwardly; neither is that circumcision, which is outward in the flesh; But he is a Jew, which is one inwardly; and circumcision is that of the heart, in the spirit, and not in the letter" (Rom. 2:28-29). Many prophecies and promises to the Jews refer to the spiritual Israel. It is decidedly wrong to offer false hopes to the Jewish nation. Physical Jews are placed on an equal basis with Gentiles in the gospel day of grace. "There is neither Jew nor Greek, there is neither bond nor free, there is neither male nor female: for ye are all one in Christ Jesus. And if ye be Christ's, then are ye Abraham's seed, and heirs according to the promise" (Gal. 3:28-29).

Literal Israel had twelve tribes. John pictures twelve thousand in each tribe. This gives the complete number, whole, every tribe included, as 144,000. The number is used as a symbol to represent spiritual Israel, the church. As 666 represents the pope of Rome, by means of contrast the 144,000 is given to delineate the true church. Grave error is made by those claiming only 144,000 (literally figuring) will be in heaven. John said, "After this I beheld, and, lo, a great multitude, **which no man could number,** of all nations, and kindreds, and people, and tongues, stood before the throne, and before the Lamb, clothed with white robes, and palms in their hands" (Rev. 7:9).

John's portrait of sealing Israel is a scene placed at the beginning of the Christian era. To "seal means to mark, stamp or ' imprint. It was a custom to stamp servants in their foreheads to distinguish ownership. John is expressing how God gathered out a people for Himself and marked them as His own in the very beginning of the Christian dispensation. He marked the true Israel as His church. Paul said, "The foundation of God standeth sure, having this seal; the Lord knoweth them that are his" (2 Tim. 2:19). Chapter fourteen of John's vision depicts God sealing His people with His name in their foreheads at the closing of the Christian era. This is a fulfillment in our day; God's church is restored in the evening of the gospel day to the same truth as was given in the morning light. True worshippers being marked with the seal of only the Father's name in their foreheads is a means of contrast to those who bear the mark of the beast. John describes this host of worshippers as those "that had gotten victory over the beast [Catholicism], and over his image [Protestantism], and over his mark, and over the number of his name [666]" (Rev. 15:2). They sang the song of Moses—a song of deliverance; and the song of the Lamb—redemption's refrain. As a child bears the likeness and name of his father, so God's children bear His image and name. It was for this Christ prayed saying, "Holy Father, keep through thine own name those who thou hast given me . . ." (John 17:11b). Paul writes, ". . . I bow my knees unto the Father of our Lord Jesus Christ, of whom the whole family in heaven and earth is named" (Eph. 3:14-15). Here is a people free from all sectarian names and creeds and following only the Lamb of God. It is interesting to note that the only name God gives the church is His own. All through the New Testament the church bears the title, "Church of God." God called a people for His Name (Acts 15:14). The church belongs to God. God thought it; Christ bought it; The Holy Spirit brought it.

To "seal" means more than just to mark or imprint. It also means to preserve or keep. This was the concern of Christ's prayer for His disciples: "I pray not that thou shouldest take them out of the world, but that thou shouldest **keep** them from the evil" (John 17:15). The illustration of sealing a fruit jar is frequently used to explain this truth. A jar may be washed, filled with good fruit, and sealed with a lid to preserve it. If the seal is broken, air gets inside and fermentation begins. In time the pressure will force the lid off and the contents are lost. Some folks are vessels washed in Christ's blood and filled with fruit of the Spirit. These souls can be preserved only by the sealing of the Holy Spirit received in a sanctifying experience. Paul said, "in whom also after that ye believed, ye were **sealed** with that Holy Spirit of promise" (Eph. 1:13). And again, "Grieve not the holy

Spirit of God, whereby ye are **sealed** unto the day of redemption" (Eph. 4:30). Individuals refusing the sanctifying grace of the Holy Spirit are as unsealed fruit jars. Sin enters their lives and causes spiritual decay. Pressures of the self-life get hot and explode. Too often professing saints "blow their top," leaving a bad odor rather than a sweet-smelling savor.

John saw the church as a great company of pure, undefiled holy saints, worshipping the Lamb of God in the evening time our gospel day. (See Rev. 14:5.) This is the ideal portrait of God's church: A holy people freed from apostasy, whole and complete, bearing the Father's name and image, following Jesus, the Lamb on Mount Zion.

CHAPTER IV

THE TEMPLE CHRIST BUILDS
(Revelation Chapter 11)

(See Picture Chart following page 32: Strip 2)

The Contemporary architecture is designed for tomorrow's world. Some thought has even been given to the style, size, and construction of buildings the scientists visualize for Mars, the moon, and outer space. However, God is always far beyond the human mind. Almost two thousand years have passed since God sent His Son to earth as the Master Builder, to build a church designed for eternity. Construction for the edifice reaches around the globe and extends beyond outer space, towering into the borders of heaven. John the Revelator discloses the Divine Builder's sketches of this temple of truth. He has heard Christ proclaim, "I will build my church; and the gates of hell shall not prevail against it" (Matt. 16:18b). While men are building bomb shelters for survival, Christ is constructing a temple bombs can never destroy. First-century records compiled in the Book of Acts give the account that "the Lord added to the church daily such as should be saved" (Acts 2:47b). This is evidence that the construction of the Lord's temple began at His first advent.

The Apostle Paul keenly visualized the spiritual edifice that Christ came to build. To the Corinthians he wrote, "For ye are the temple of the living God" (2 Cor. 6:16). To the Ephesians he explained, "ye are no more strangers and foreigners, but fellowcitizens with the saints, and of the household of God; and are built upon the foundation of the apostles and prophets, Jesus Christ himself being the chief corner stone; in whom all the building fitly framed together groweth unto an holy temple in the

Lord: In whom ye also are builded together for an habitation of God through the Spirit" (Eph. 2:19-22).

Long before excavation begins, the architect carefully designs, plans, measures, and calculates the construction cost. This is very true of the Divine Architect. Before the world of time began God designed the church, and knew that the purchase price would be the blood of "the Lamb slain from the foundation of the world" (Rev. 13:8b). The church is not an afterthought with God; not, as some suppose, a secondary plan inaugurated when Christ was rejected by the Jews. Calvary was not a defeat; the day Christ paid the purchase price for His church, He accomplished what He came to do at the first advent.

Blueprints for the Temple

When Mount Sinai was aflame with the glory of God and Moses trembled to hear the voice of the Almighty, a blueprint was given for the erection of the tabernacle in Israel. God gave specific instructions to Moses warning against any deviations from the plan. Moses could not comprehend that the hand of God was also sketching blueprints for the New Testament church. The literal tabernacle of Moses was to serve as a miniature sketch of the spiritual temple of Christ. The blueprints God gave to Moses were very unique. There had never been a structure built by this pattern before. When the tabernacle was completed, the light, portable building would not begin to compare with the glistening marble walls or the great granite blocks in the temple of Diana or the Parthenon at Athens. Neither could it compare in vastness with the colossal temple of the sun at ancient Heliopolis, for Moses built a tabernacle scarcely larger than a two-room cottage.

All truth has its roots in prophecy. Every doctrine of Christianity can be traced in the Old Testament shadows where the Scriptures are rich with prophecies of the church. The requirements and furnishings of the ancient tabernacle foreshadow great articles of faith in the temple of truth.

The Temple Foundation

Excavation for the temple structure began when John the Baptist came preaching repentance. His cry, "Prepare ye the way of the Lord, make his paths straight" (Luke 3:4b), was to clear away the debris of sin, probe into the consciences of men, dig deep into their souls, and remove erroneous beliefs.

Christ's acclamation, "Repent: for the kingdom of heaven is at hand" (Matt. 4:17), marks the time construction began. As Christ preached the great truth of the kingdom, proclaimed doctrine with divine authority, and confirmed His words with mighty deeds, the foundation took form as the solid rock. Paul speaks a great truth when he asserts, "Other foundation can no man lay than that is laid, which is Jesus Christ" (1 Cor. 3:11). The Divine Builder carefully selected the apostles as lively stones to become a part of the foundation with Him. Peter describes the formation of the temple as a great host of lively stones cemented together with the mortar of love. He writes in his first epistle, "Ye also, as lively stones, are built up a spiritual house, an holy priesthood, to offer up spiritual sacrifices, acceptable to God by Jesus Christ" (1 Pet. 2:5).

The Temple Door

Observing specifications for Moses' tabernacle, it is noted that there is only one door providing a means of entrance. This was to typify Christ as the only door to His church. When Jesus spoke of being the door He used the metaphor of a sheepfold. The Palestinian shepherd led his sheep at night into a fold of safety. The fold had only one entrance which was simply an open place in the wall. The sheep were counted as they entered. When they were all safely inside, the shepherd himself lay down across the opening; nothing and no one could get in or out except by the shepherd.

The Roman Catholic religion maintains that the pope is the means of entrance into the church and admission is granted to those who merit it by ritual and good works. Protestantism copies this error with the false claim of the clergy assuming authority for opening the doors of the church and granting admission to individuals who gain entrance by observing certain religious rites. It is true that one enters the religions of men by men as the door; but a divine religion has only the divine door. Jesus said, "I am the door: by me if any man enter in, he shall be saved" (John 10:9). Admission into Christ's temple is granted only to those who come by faith through the blood of Jesus Christ. Our Lord also said, "He that entereth not by the door into the sheep-fold, but climbeth up some other way, the same is a thief and a robber" (John 10:1).

The High Priest of the Temple

The comparison between type and antitype is amazing. No one can study types and shadows with sincerity and not conclude that God is truly the Author of the Scriptures. The ancient priest, Aaron, dimly shadowed the glory of the High Priest, Jesus Christ, in the New Testament Israel of God. Christ divinely fulfilled every requirement of the priestly office. First, the priest must be divinely appointed; Christ is the appointed One of the Father (Heb. 5:5). Second, the priest must be pure, not defiling himself by touching any dead thing, and must marry only a virgin, never a divorced woman, a harlot, or a widow. Christ is holy; there is no defilement of the dead works of iniquity in Him. He has but one bride, the church, and she is not a harlot married to the creeds and doctrines of men. Third, a priest must be physically perfect; Christ was both spiritually and physically perfect. Fourth, the high priest wore on his shoulders and breastplate beautiful gems and onyx stones inscribed with the names of all the twelve tribes of Israel. This is indicative of Christ, our Advocate, who bears the names of all spiritual Israel upon His shoulders lifting them to the Father. True saints are as precious gems carried close to the heart of Christ. Every tribe and nation is near to His heart. Not only the lionlike Judah is represented but even Reuben, unstable as water, is carried before God. The miter of the priest was of glistening gold engraved with raised letters of "Holiness unto the Lord." Thus, the priest not only represented the tribes of Israel to God but also represented God to the people. All of the foregoing reaches complete fulfillment in the Christ.

The Temple Furnishings

God's blueprint to Moses included seven pieces of furniture for the tabernacle. Each furnishing is a type of Christ. It is intriguing to observe Christ carefully providing each piece of furniture for His temple.

1. The Brazen Altar.

Just inside the court of Moses' place of worship stood a large altar made of brass. When the sinful Israelite came to worship, the priest at the entrance of the court received his sacrifice, and laid it upon the brass network of the altar. After the sacrificial animal was carefully examined, it was tied with cords to the horns of the altar. The sin-burdened Israelite cut the animal's throat, and the priest hastily caught the blood to sprinkle it upon God's altar. This was a very important part of the ceremony because only blood could atone for the soul. The sinner laid his hands upon the dying animal, believing that when it died his sins died with it.

From a tiny acorn which God himself made, a tree grew in the soil of the earth created by His hand. When it was full grown, it was hewn down to build the altar for Christ's temple. The altar, built in the form of a cross, held the Lamb of God by the cords of man's sin. Guilty sinners pierced His side with the sharp spear of evil transgressions, breaking His heart; and the fountain of blood and water ushered forth. The blood from Immanuel's veins was sprinkled upon the altar of God to justify man before his Creator. By faith we, as sinners, touch the Lamb of God and believe that when He died, our sins died with Him. No one escapes the blood of Jesus. Some men may have it on their hands like Pilate; others have it upon their heads like the

Jews who cried for Christ's blood to be upon them and their children; there are those who trample it under their feet like Herod;
many like Judas have it upon their conscience; but blessed is the
man who has it upon his heart to cover his sins and clothe his
naked soul. Eternity will be none too long to offer praise unto
the "Lamb of God, which taketh away the sin of the world"
(John 1:29), making our justification possible by His own blood!

2. The Laver.

In Israel's court of worship between the brazen altar and the
tabernacle stood a laver or large basin of water. Priests were
commanded to wash both hands and feet before entering the
house of worship. Christ also provided a fountain of cleansing at
the entrance of His temple. It is not enough that man is justified
through the atonement. He must become a new creature; old
things must pass away and all things must become new. To
Nicodemus Jesus said, "Except a man be born of water and of
the Spirit, he cannot enter the kingdom of God" (John 3:5). Paul
speaks of the Word being as water cleansing the church ". . .
with the washing of water by the **word**, that he might present it
to himself a glorious church, not having spot, or wrinkle" (Eph.
5:26b-27a). Jesus said to the disciples, "Now ye are clean
through the **word** which I have spoken unto you" (John 15:3).
This washing is a work of **regeneration**, a **new birth**. The old
life gone and a new being is created. As it was written that a
priest must wash before entering the holy place of worship "lest
he die," even so we cannot enter God's temple, the church, without a cleansing, a regeneration, the new birth. Christ alone is our
Laver of washing for the soul.

3. The Golden Candlestick.

Entering the sanctuary of Moses' tabernacle, one's attention
was captured by a beautiful golden candlestick. It was made of a
talent of gold; its approximate value was **$27,375.00**. Shedding
its beams of light throughout the room, it stood alone—the only
light. Its number of seven candles denoted complete perfection.

This is an exquisite symbol of Christ who is the perfect and only light in His temple. Little was this significant truth realized when Jesus exclaimed, "I am the light of the world; he that followeth me shall not walk in darkness, but shall have the light of life" (John 8:12). The Christ also uttered, "And this is the condemnation, that light is come into the world, and men loved darkness rather than light, because their deeds were evil" (John 3:19). Jesus carefully lit each gospel truth and established the Christian faith of gospel light. Truly John has written, "In him was life; and the life was the light of men" (John 1:4).

4. The Table of Shewbread.

In the holy place of Moses' tabernacle, opposite the golden candlestick, stood a golden-covered table. On the table twelve loaves of bread were placed each Sabbath Day. There was a loaf for each of the twelve tribes of Israel. Here was "bread for the small tribe of Benjamin as well as for royal Judah." Frankincense was also laid with the bread. When fresh loaves were brought, the former loaves were eaten by the priests in the holy place while the incense was burned on the golden altar.

In Christ's temple, the bread was not forgotten. Christ Himself became bread for every tribe and nation—not one is excluded. Hear Christ saying, "I am the bread of life; he that cometh to me shall never hunger" (John 6:35a). "I am the living bread which came down from heaven; if any man eat this bread, he shall live for ever: and the bread that I will give is my flesh, which I will give for the life of the world" (John 6:51).

Remembering the priests of Israel eating the bread sprinkling the blood on the holy altar, and offering incense, a vivid picture is drawn of the Lord's last supper with His disciples. There they ate broken bread, a symbol of His body, and also drank the wine, a symbol of His blood. To this was added the sweet incense of the High Priestly prayer in Gethsemane. Only as we are partakers of Christ, the True Bread, can we have communion with the Father. The symbolism of the unleavened loaf is most interesting. The loaf was round—like a circle which has no beginning or ending; Christ is the Alpha and Omega. It was without leaven to reveal a Christ without sin or carnality. The broken loaf was a symbol of our Lord's crucified body. There was a Jewish custom of having a member of the family hide a piece of unleavened bread at the passover time. This was a shadow of the hidden body of our Lord in the grave.

Christ carried the meaning of the loaf further to express that the church is the body of Christ. Christians are gathered as grains of wheat from many fields of life. As chaff is removed from wheat and grain is changed into flour, so Christians have their sin taken away, and surrender to be crushed, changed, converted into one body—the Body of Christ. A second change is made when the bread is placed in an oven to bake. It is a chemical change and the very nature of the grain is transformed. In like manner Christians not only experience salvation when the chaff of sin is removed; they also know the power of the Spirit's flame burning in the soul, transforming their very nature by a sanctifying grace. The church, too, must know the joy of being unleavened bread. Only as the church is crucified, broken, and given to the hungry souls of men, will the world see the true Body of Christ revealed.

5. The Golden Altar.

Between the golden candlestick and the table of shewbread a golden altar was placed near the veil between the holy place an the holy of holies of the Jewish tabernacle. Here incense was burned and blood was sprinkled. Only by this altar is communion with God possible. While the priest ate the sacred bread, he must do so in the offering of blood at this altar while the incense of prayer and devotion was lifted to God. The brazen altar is closely related to this second altar of gold. The fire for the golden altar was live coals from the altar of justification. This fire was divinely sent from God. The same blood shed at the first altar was carried to this second place of sacrifice. A diligent study of the book of Hebrews makes all these symbols become

animated. As the blood of Christ justifies the soul, it also sancti-
fies the believer. "Wherefore Jesus also, that he might sanctify
the people with his own blood, suffered without [outside] the
gate" (Heb. 13:12). Christ provided this altar of **sanctification**
while praying in Gethsemane, "Sanctify them through thy truth;
thy word is truth" (John 17:17). But the altar was only valid
when Christ sprinkled the blood from Calvary upon it.

How precious is the golden experience of the sanctified
life! As truly as Moses was commanded to erect two altars, two
rooms, two veils, and make two applications of blood (one at the
brazen altar and one at the golden altar), Christ also provides in
His temple for a twofold experience of the Christian faith.

6. The Temple Veil.

Two veils were placed in Moses' tabernacle. The first was
at the entrance to the holy place and the second hung at the entrance to the holy of holies. Each veil is a symbol of Christ. Only
through Him do we gain entrance to His temple. The brazen altar
and the laver stood before the first veil to signify the necessity of
justification and new birth before entering Christ's church. The
second veil was erected between the holy place and the holy of
holies. This veil was rent in two from top to bottom by invisible
hands at the death of Jesus. That Christ is typified by the veil is
plainly stated by the author of Hebrews: "Having therefore,
brethren, boldness to enter into the holiest by the blood of Jesus,
by a new and living way, which he hath consecrated for us,
through the veil, that is to say his flesh . . ." (Heb. 10:19-20). As
they were rending our Lord's body, an entrance was made for
man to approach the very throne of God through Him.

7. The Ark of the Covenant.

Entering through the veil into the holy of holies, the most
peculiar, most sacred and impressive, and the most significant
piece of furniture is seen. Here stands only one furnishing—the
ark of the covenant. It is the beautiful golden chest which serves
as a receptacle for the two tables of stone inscribed with the Ten

Commandments, for a golden bowl of manna, and for Aaron's rod that budded (Heb. 9). A large, flat piece of pure gold provides a top (cover or lid) for the golden chest. This is called the mercy seat. Here the priest poured blood on the Day of Atonement. Two angelic figures were fashioned, one at each end of the mercy seat with wings touching in the center, thus forming a canopy. The angelic creatures were named Justice and Mercy. God had told Moses that He would meet and commune with man above the mercy seat between the cherubim. On Atonement Day the high priest entered into this holy of holies. He poured blood of the sacrifice upon the altar, and for the space of three hours he stood in the darkness making intercession for Israel. According to Jewish tradition the Shekinah then shone upon the mercy seat. The high priest returned to the waiting assembly of the Israelites and lifting up his arms cried, "It is finished." Thus atonement was acclaimed for Israel's transgressions.

The position of the temple furniture formed a cross. The brazen altar formed the foot, and the ark of the covenant made the head. The laver and golden altar were set between. The golden candlestick and the table of shewbread formed the crosspiece. Each time the priest carried the blood in worship, God saw the blood spilled in the form of a cross.

Everyone has the blood of Christ somewhere.

> Some on their heads—as Jews
> Some on their hands—as Pilate
> Some on their feet—as soldiers
> Some on their conscience—as Judas
> Some on their hearts—as forgiveness

The depth of meaning in all this shadow picture of type is beyond human comprehension. The most awe-inspiring room of Christ's temple is this holy of holies, the very throne of God. Christ provided His covenant "not in tables of stone, but in fleshly tables of the heart" (2 Cor. 3: 3b). Christ established a new covenant saying, "For this is my blood of the new testament, which is shed for many for the remission of sins" (Matt. 26:28). The New Testament fulfills the old law which was sprinkled with the blood of calves and goats. Christ's covenant is sanctified with the sacred blood of Jesus Christ. Christ is also that hidden manna of His own temple. He, Himself, is the rod typified by Aaron's rod that budded. This is a symbol of His resurrection. Aaron's rod was dead, but became alive, budded, and bore fruit as almonds (Num. 17:8). Hear Christ saying, "I am he that liveth, and was dead; and behold, I am alive for evermore" (Rev. 1:18a). He who became the first fruits of them that slept also provides resurrection for all men both spiritually and bodily. We, too, were as dead as Aaron's rod, cut off from God by our sin. Christ came to bring us life. We must bud, blossom, and bring forth fruit.

Most precious of all, Christ is the pure gold mercy seat of His temple. Upon Him all the sin of the world must be laid. On the day of crucifixion, Christ as our High Priest took His own blood and poured it out before God in mercy to make atonement for our sins. The sky became black at twelve o'clock noon. For three hours our great High Priest interceded in the dense darkness. At three o'clock in the afternoon, with outstretched arms, our High Priest uttered, "It is finished" (John 19:30). Then He died. Atonement was made! The light which again appeared was as the Shekinah between God's justice and mercy.

It must be called to our attention that each piece of furniture in Moses' tabernacle was by God's command equipped with fixtures and rods for carrying. When Israel moved from one place to another, the priests were commanded to place the rods on their shoulders and transport the sacred furnishings as well as the tabernacle itself. It is the duty of God's ministers today, as we travel through the wilderness of sin, to carry the sacred doctrines of Christ's temple, even the truth of the church itself, to every generation.

The Dedication of Christ's Temple

As one parable alone is insufficient to describe the kingdom of God, so one earthly temple is inadequate to typify the temple which Christ builds.

When Joshua led the Israelites into Canaan, the tabernacle was erected at Shiloh. Because of Israel's disobedience in later years, God forsook Shiloh. Even the ark of the covenant was stolen by the Philistines but later returned. At the time David became king, the tabernacle was at Gibeon and the ark was in Jerusalem. David greatly desired to build a temple for God; however, David was engaged in war during many of his years as king. There was no time to build a temple. God also desired the temple to be built by a man of peace rather than a man of war and bloodshed. When David's youngest son by Bathsheba was born, he was named Solomon, which means "peaceable." David anticipated that his son would reign in peace. David made plans and purchased many materials for constructing a temple. Solomon was approximately twenty years of age when he became king. He endeavored to fulfill the great dreams of his father, David, who died soon after Solomon was anointed to Israel. It was when Solomon went to Gibeon to worship God appeared in a dream and bade him ask for anything he chose. His choice for wisdom and an understanding heart was granted. The peace David had fought to establish was of great value to Solomon. Not only did he devote a great measure of time and effort to build the Temple, but neighboring kings and territories assisted in preparing materials for the construction. All the materials for the great structure were hewn, squared, or planed before they were brought to Jerusalem. "There was neither hammer nor axe nor any tool of iron heard in the house, while it was in building" (1 Kings 6: 7b). This was a shadow-type of Christ building His church. All "lively stones" for the spiritual house are skillfully hewn, leveled, and cut to size before they can be built into the eternal structure. This is accomplished as the Spirit silently performs His work in the souls of men.

There is an old story of an ancient sculptor who purchased a crude stone at a high cost. Daily he chipped away at the black covering of the oddly shaped stone. One day a traveler passing by inquired, "What are you doing with that stone?" "There is an angel in this stone and I must free him," replied the sculptor. To the traveler's eye there was not even the slightest figure of an angel. "Many blows must be wielded and numerous chips must fall before you can see the angel," the sculptor planned. Years later the traveler returned. Looking toward the once ugly stone his eyes fell upon the carving of a beautiful white angel with outspread wings. The angel had been in the stone all the time, but it took the skilled hands of a sculptor to unveil it.

The Great Sculptor has purchased many "lively stones" at the cost of His own blood. They, too, were black, ugly, and oddly shaped. How skillfully the Sculptor labors with strange tools. Frequently He uses the cutting edge of disappointment or the chisels of trial, pain, and affliction. There are times when even a blow of sorrow and death help to wrought His perfect work. How glorious to behold the "saint" which the Master Sculptor has set free!

For seven years Solomon and his workmen labored to construct the Temple. Furnishings were brought from Gibeon and the ark of the covenant was brought from the place where it had been sheltered temporarily in the city of David. The grandeur of Solomon's Temple is beyond description. Its vast dimensions, towering pillars, and glistening gold throughout presented a glorious sight to behold. All this was but a dim shadow of the magnificent church Christ builds! The day of dedication for Solomon's Temple found the priests coming carrying the ark of the covenant. As honor and praise were offered with Israel's sacrificial lamb, God descended upon the Temple as a great cloud. His glory filled the Temple in such great measure that the priests could not minister therein.

Solomon's Temple and all its glory were destined to fade and pass away. The Temple served only as a negative of the real picture of Christ's church. The Master Builder established a firm foundation of solid rock. High massive walls of salvation rest upon the Chief Cornerstone and apostles of the Lamb. Noble saints of all ages are stalwart pillars. Each living stone is engraved with the image and beauty of Christ. The Divine Builder furnished His temple with great doctrines of holy splendor. The structure was consecrated with His own blood. He arose from the dead to minister in His temple as great High Priest. For forty days He remained on earth to present infallible proof of the resurrection. (This number "forty" appears many times in the Bible and indicates a judgment number, a time of testing and proving.) Before Jesus ascended to His heavenly throne, He commanded the disciples to tarry in Jerusalem until the Holy Spirit came. Ten days were spent by the early Christians in an upper room of prayer. They offered praise and honor to Christ, the great Sacrifice. These ten days climaxed with Pentecost—the day of dedication for Christ's temple. God had honored Solomon's Temple with His presence as the ark was carried in; to honor the temple of His Son, the Holy Spirit came to abide. Thus the church became the habitation of God through the Spirit. Far greater than the cloud of glory in Solomon's day was the rushing mighty wind, the cloven tongues of fire, a baptism of the Holy Spirit on every living stone! So powerful was the Spirit in their midst that the apostles could no longer minister only in the temple. They hastened to minister the gospel to every tribe and nation.

Pentecost was a great day in the Jewish calendar. It was sometimes called "Feast of Harvest." How significant for God to choose this day for the first fruits of spiritual harvest; three thousand souls were added to the church. Pentecost will never be repeated any more than Jesus will be born a babe in Bethlehem again. The Spirit's coming was not a transient affair. He came to abide, is in the world today, and will remain until the end of time when Christ appears. So great is the Spirit's coming that each Christian may still share in the dedication day of Christ's temple.

We are as individual temples of the Holy Spirit and His power fills the sanctuary of the soul; thus we, too, share in the dedication of Christ's temple.

The Desecration of the Temple

Remembering that Daniel depicts four earthly kingdoms in sharp contrast with the kingdom of God, it is worthy of note that four earthly temples are drawn in direct comparison with the divine temple which Christ builds. Attention is focused here on the third temple of contrast.

After Solomon's Temple lay in ruins and the Jews were carried away into Babylonian captivity, Jeremiah's prophecies were diligently searched to learn when Jerusalem would be restored. Daniel became much concerned about the passage which promised a restoration after seventy years of captivity (Jer. 25:11-12). The angel Gabriel explained to Daniel that many Old Testament prophecies have a literal and a spiritual fulfillment (See Daniel chap. 9.) After seventy literal years of captivity the Jews would be released to rebuild Jerusalem and reconstruct their temple. The seventy weeks of years were to be spiritually fulfilled. (Seventy weeks would mean seventy times seven or four hundred and ninety days, equal to four hundred and ninety years in prophetic time.)

Daniel had witnessed the end of those seventy years in Babylon. In the year 457 B.C. King Cyrus gave the decree to rebuild Jerusalem. Nehemiah and Ezra led the Jews in reconstructing the holy city. Cyrus appointed Zerubbabel, prince of Judah, as governor of the colony of returned exiles. It is interesting to observe that Zerubbabel is mentioned by Matthew in the direct line of ancestry of our Lord (Matt. 1:12). During the administration of Zerubbabel, the Temple was rebuilt in Jerusalem. The plan of Solomon's Temple was followed but projected on a scale of far less magnificence. Many of the former temple vessels were restored but the holy of holies remained an empty room; the ark of the covenant had disappeared.

Near the end of the Grecian kingdom, the tyrant, Antiochus Epiphanes, waged war against Israel. This selfish, wicked ruler was determined to destroy the Jews. Thousands of pious Jews, who regarded their sanctuary more precious than their lives, died in the conflict, endeavoring to preserve the temple from Gentile defilement. Antiochus desecrated Zerubbabel's Temple by overthrowing the sacred vessels and even offering swine on the sacred altars. He killed the priests and pious Jews. A command was given for the daily sacrifice to cease and for sacrifices to be offered to heathen gods. This was described as the "abomination of desolation" (Dan. 11:31). Antiochus was defeated by Judas Maccabeus (the Hammer) who beat down the Gentile invader and established Jewish independence which lasted for about one hundred and fifty years.

The spiritual fulfillment of the seventy weeks is of far greater significance. Daniel said these weeks were to reach to the "Messiah, the Prince," our Lord Jesus. He would deliver souls from the captivity of sin and construct a spiritual temple. His new covenant was confirmed with many. This beautiful temple, his church, was erected in glorious splendor. John saw this holy structure in his vision on the Isle of Patmos (Rev. 11). The angel gave a prophecy that the holy temple of our Lord would be desecrated and trodden under foot for a long period of time. The prophecy came to fulfillment during the period called the Dark Ages. Roman Catholic powers endeavored to destroy the true church. Many sincere Christians were put to death when they refused to see the sanctuary of truth defiled.

The Roman teaching first attempted to pillage the temple by overthrowing the altar of "justification by faith." Roman Catholics maintain salvation is by works. Our human works are as swine on God's altar. Only the blood of the Lamb will suffice. The doctrine of atonement through Christ alone was adulterated by the claim of priests who appointed themselves as mediators for the souls of men. Further plundering the temple of truth, the laver of regeneration (the doctrine of new birth) was substituted with a baptismal font. Roman Catholicism teaches that a child is born again by sprinkling for baptism. An effort was made to remove the first veil of Christ's temple when Rome claimed the Catholic church to be the only means of entrance into salvation. The golden candlestick of gospel light was eclipsed; the Dark Ages came to pass, multitudes stumbled back into heathen superstition and the blackness of sin. The table of shewbread was confiscated by the Roman hierarchy as Bibles were chained; only priests and monks had access to the Scriptures. Thus a spiritual famine for the Bread of Life prevailed everywhere.

The doctrine of the golden altar of sanctification was mutilated; Romanism proclaims holy days, holy ashes, holy water, etc., but not holy people. In a daring manner the pope claims to be the veil of entrance to the throne of God. Most sacrilegious of all, the pontiff seats himself upon canonical laws of human origin, asserts that he is the "holy father" presiding over the ark of the covenant with power to forgive sins! Thus Paul's prophecy of the "man of sin" is fulfilled when it is written, ". . . and that man of sin be revealed, the son of perdition; who opposeth and exalteth himself above all that is called God, or that is worshipped; so that he as God sitteth in the temple of God, shewing himself that he is God (2 Thess. 2:3b-4). The man who exercises authority in St. Peter's at Rome vindicates that he is infallible. His triple crown signifies his claim—"king of heaven, king of earth, and king of hell." He assumes power over the saints who are dead and over all souls on earth—power to release or damn in purgatory. Further prophecies will reveal the cleansing of the sanctuary, the true temple restored, and everlasting peace established.

Measuring Christ's Temple

Carried away in the Spirit, John visions the temple of God. He is given a rod and bidden by an angel to measure the temple. This could not have been an earthly structure. There was no temple on the Isle of Patmos. The rod was the word of God, as it is expressed in Psalm 23, "Thy rod and thy staff, they comfort me." Only a divine scale of measure could be used to determine the dimensions of a spiritual structure. John was bidden to measure the altar. The altar is the place where the sacrifice was slain and the blood was shed. To measure how far the blood reaches on the altar of the New Testament church is to measure the atonement. The blood reaches back to Adam and forward to the last soul that is given birth. The blood of bulls and goats could not save the soul. If that had been possible, Jesus would not have needed to die. Old Testament sacrifices are only as postdated checks which were not valid until Christ deposited the blood in heaven's bank. Christ is the one and only Saviour of all the world. As John is bidden to omit the court of the Gentiles, Herod's temple is referred to in striking contrast with Christ's temple.

After Herod the Great became ruler of the Jews, he desired to gain their favor by rebuilding and beautifying Zerubbabel's Temple. Herod was not a Jew. He, as a politician, must also please the Gentiles. When he reconstructed the Temple, he failed to build according to the Jewish pattern and included a court of the Gentiles. When using an earthly temple as a type of the spiritual temple, man's addition must be omitted. Only circumcised Jews who kept the law were permitted to worship in the Jewish Temple. Likewise, only spiritual Jews who have had circumcision of the heart and keep the law of Christ are permitted the rite of worship in Christ's church. Here is reference to Paul's words, "He is not a Jew, which is one outwardly; neither is that circumcision, which is outward in the flesh: But he is a Jew, which is one inwardly; and circumcision is that of the heart, in the spirit, and not in the letter" (Rom. 2:28-29a). There are no uncircumcised hearts in the church of God. Christians are all included in Christ's temple as the spiritual Israel of God. They are Abraham's seed by faith.

Herod's Temple was constructed of white-and-green-spotted marble. Josephus says the stones were twenty-four feet broad, fifty feet long and sixteen feet thick. Its construction began sixteen years before the birth of Jesus. Within the walls of this edifice Mary and Joseph dedicated the Christ as a babe. Its high golden dome must have glistened in the sun as Jesus saw it for the first time when He approached Jerusalem at the age of twelve. His inaugural act of entering the public ministry was the cleansing of this Temple. Many miracles of our Lord took place in the courts of this house of worship. It is significant to observe that the final act of our Lord's public ministry was the cleansing of the Temple again during His final week of earthly life. It was the veil of this Temple that was rent in twain the hour Christ died.

Jesus prophesied the destruction of Herod's Temple (Matt. 24:1-2). Looking over Jerusalem, the Master wept. The Jews had persecuted, stoned, scourged and slain God's prophets. The Lord knew they soon would crucify God's own Son. The blood of the innocent was already upon their hands and they would cry for the blood of Christ to be upon them and their children. Looking over their city, the Temple met the Master's eyes as He uttered, "Behold, your house is left unto you desolate" (Matt. 23:38). Again he said, ". . . There shall not be left here one stone upon another that shall not be thrown" (Matt. 24:2b). Jesus also explained that the generation of that day would not pass until all these things should be fulfilled. He reminded his disciples of the "abomination of desolation" spoken of by Daniel; and they understood that he prophesied a more terrible tribulation for the Jews who would crucify him, than had been experienced by the Jews in the days of Antiochus Epiphanes. The Greek tyrant had desecrated Zerubbabel's Temple; but Jesus spoke of Titus, the Roman prince, who would utterly destroy Herod's Temple. Describing that great tribulation to fall upon Jerusalem as judgment from God for crucifying the Christ, Jesus said that the disciples should flee when the armies began to encamp about the city. They were bidden to leave in haste. If they were on the housetop, they should not take time to go down into their houses for their possessions; or if they were in the fields, they should make immediate flight because once the city was besieged, there would be no escape. Christ exhorted His followers to pray their flight would not be on the Sabbath day; the city gates were closed and a Sabbath day's journey was very short. They should desire the flight be not in the winter because travel would be very difficult. Jesus remembered that there would be women with children and others pregnant with child. To the women who lamented as our Lord was being led to crucifixion, He said, "weep not for me, but weep for yourselves, and for your children" (Luke 23:28b).

About forty years after the crucifixion, all these prophecies came to pass. The Christians remembered the Lord's warning and fled when the armies were surrounding Jerusalem. The armies of Titus became the scourge of God for judgment upon the wicked nation that had rejected the Christ. Horror reigned inside the city. There was no escape. Some became insane. Women were known to boil the flesh of their own children for food. The Temple court was used as a fortress. When the Roman armies entered the city, they found many already dead. Almost a million and a half Jews were slain. Some were killed with the sword; others were burned; many were crucified until no more wood could be found to make crosses. Blood ran in Jerusalem like a river. This was the time of Jacob's trouble. Many people expect this great tribulation, which has already taken place, to occur in the future.

Roman soldiers with eagle banners entered into the holy of holies and offered sacrifices to Emperor Vespasian. The Temple was then set on fire. After all that was combustible was consumed, the walls were thrown down; even the foundations were dug up and Zion was plowed as a field. The Jews sowed a cross and were made to reap crosses. They filled the cup of God's wrath and it spilled upon them. Thus the ancient Jewish sacrifices were abolished and the Christian dispensation was established. Daniel's prophecy was fulfilled. He said that the Messiah should "cause the sacrifice and the oblation to cease" (Dan.

9:27). Today a heathen mosque is erected on the site where Herod's Temple once stood.

Unlike the temples of men, Christ builds a temple that even gates of hell cannot destroy. Its foundation standeth sure. The walls of salvation are impregnable. The living stones are the eternal souls of the righteous. When John prophesies concerning the host of Gentiles (uncircumcised-Roman Catholics) desecrating Christ's temple, he hastens to say that God will give power to two witnesses who will prophesy for one thousand, two hundred and 60 days in sackcloth. This period is equal in time to the forty-two months that the city was to be downtrodden. The two witnesses were symbolized by olive trees and candlesticks.

From a shadow picture in Zechariah 4, it is learned that the olive tree is an emblem of living oil being constantly supplied to an eternal lamp. Oil is a symbol of the **Spirit**. We have often repeated the phrase, "Thou anointest my head with oil" (Ps. 23:5). We use oil to anoint the sick as a symbol of the Spirit upon them. There is no question that the Holy Spirit is God's Witness in the earth. The candlestick is a lamp to give forth light. A favorite verse of Scripture expresses, "Thy word is a lamp unto my feet, and a light unto my path" (Ps. 119:105). Thus the **Word** is an anointed witness. Both the Spirit and the Word testify and bear witness which is eternal. What oil is to a lamp, the Spirit is to the Word. This promise meant much to the saints during the Dark Ages. It brought the comfort of the abiding presence of God's Spirit; hungry hearts would be sustained in days of spiritual famine, for the Word, the living Bread, could not be destroyed. The church of Rome endeavored numbers of times to annihilate the Word by burning the Scriptures. They determined to extinguish the Spirit by martyring saints; but the Spirit and Word continued to witness. Sometimes they were found in the catacombs of Rome. Often they appeared in sackcloth amid the sanctuary of a few solitary hearts, but always they were preserving truth. Though in the wilderness, the church was protected, nourished, and sustained by these divine agents of God—the **Spirit** and the **Word**.

The Temple Is Restored

The given prophecy of 1,260 years expired with the ushering in of the sixteenth-century Reformation. Released from the wilderness, the church again comes into public view. The Spirit and the Word are referred to as prophets. Their divine authority is symbolized as having "power to shut heaven, that it rain not in the days of their prophecy: and have power over waters to turn them to blood, and to smite the earth with all plagues, as often as they will" (Rev. 11:6). It was Elijah who shut up heaven so that it did not rain, but rain also came by his prayer at God's appointed time after three and one-half years of drought. The reference is clear. As God preserved and fed Elijah in the wilderness, the church was nurtured and preserved during the spiritual famine. At God's appointed time the church also came out of her wilderness, and the showers of spiritual blessings flowed as truth of the Reformation was proclaimed. Moses was God's servant while Israel was in Egypt. The Egyptians held God's people in bondage, but in due time God delivered them by Moses and sent plagues upon Egypt. God permitted true Christians to be held in the bondage of Catholic Rome, but the day came for the Word to deliver them and plagues were sent upon Papal Rome. Rome lost her supremacy and no longer ruled the world.

The Spirit and Word were especially active near the end of the 1,260 years of spiritual bondage. God had miraculously preserved His church during the Dark Ages. Medieval Christians who refused to worship the beast were known in different countries by various titles as Lollards, Leonists, Cathari, Lombards, Vaudois, Poor men of Lyons, Waldenses and Albigenses. These were despised by Catholic Rome and branded as "heretics." Forerunners of the Reformation such as Jerome of Prague, John Huss, John Wycliffe, Savanarola and others were endued with great power by the Spirit and the Word.

The open break with the Catholic church came when Martin Luther declared himself opposed to Catholicism and formed the first Protestant creed in A.D. 1530. This marked a definite beginning for the restoration of the temple of truth. The down-trodden state of the church had ended. Leaving the bondage of Romanism, spiritual Babylon, the true children of God returned to rebuild the spiritual Jerusalem and to restore the holy temple, Christ's church. The restoration began with the re-establishment of the altar of "justification by faith." Catholics maintained salvation by works but Martin Luther proclaimed, "The just shall live by faith" (Rom. 1:17b). He boldly preached, "For by grace are ye saved through faith; and that not of yourselves: it is the gift of God: not of works, lest any man should boast" (Eph. 2:8-9). Luther translated the Scriptures into the German language. Thus the "Word" became very active in restoring truth revealed by the "Spirit."

Next to be restored was the truth of regeneration, symbolized by the laver of washing at the entrance of the Jewish temple. Catholics taught that new birth was experienced by baptism. Primitive Catholics believed in immersion and taught that sin was cleansed by this ordinance. Understanding that they were to live above sin after baptism, this so-called sacrament was delayed until old age. They were instructed to believe that a second baptism was unlawful; therefore to sin after baptism was to forfeit pardon. Even Constantine, the first Christian emperor, deferred his baptism until very late in life. It is easily understood that many times people waited until immersion was not possible, because of critical illness with death near. It was reasoned that if immersion washed away sins, it would be better to sprinkle a little water rather than none upon dying persons. This was called "clinical baptism" or "baptism for the sick." At first it was required that persons thus baptized, who recovered, were to have another baptism by immersion. Later the pope claimed power to forgive sins. This changed the entire picture for Catholics. Now they would be baptized by sprinkling as infants; any sins after baptism would be forgiven by the pontiff.

Zwingli, a great reformer from Switzerland, denounced baptism as a means of regeneration. John Calvin, founder of

Calvinism, claimed baptism was only a seal or sign of grace. He maintained that infant baptism was only for children of Christian parents. It was the Anabaptists, followers who broke ranks with Luther and Calvin, who demanded a reestablishment of apostolic Christianity concerning baptism and regeneration. They first attacked infant baptism by declaring it was anti-Christian, unscriptural, and a mere invention of man. They insisted there must be a "believer's baptism." Our Lord taught by precept and example a necessity of knowledge before baptism. It is written, "Then Peter said unto them, Repent, and be baptized every one of you in the name of Jesus Christ for the remission of sins, and ye shall receive the gift of the Holy Ghost" (Acts 2:38). Anabaptists receive their name from the words, "again-baptized" or "rebaptized." They restored the truth that regeneration is not by baptism but by a new birth, fellowship with God in the Spirit. This doctrine was such a revolutionary change that it brought persecution from both Catholics and Protestants. Thousands gave their lives to establish again the laver of Christ who washes sins away in His own blood. These are dead physically, but their spirit still lives. Baptism is valid only after one has died to sin, been buried with Christ, and resurrected to a newness of life in Him. "Therefore we are buried with him by baptism into death: that like as Christ was raised up from the dead by the glory of the Father, even so we also should walk in newness of life" (Rom. 6:4). It is just as absurd for a person who has not died to sin to be baptized as it is to have a funeral for someone who has not died. True baptism is the outer testimony of an inner work of faith.

Sincere Christians were as eager to restore the temple of Christ as liberated Jews had been to rebuild Zerubbabel's Temple, after Antiochus had ruthlessly defiled it. With the passing of the period of the Dark Ages, the golden candlestick of Christ's temple again bestowed light. God used a group of Christians called Friends or Quakers to revive again the flame of truth that the Divine Being speaks directly to the heart of every man, the

priesthood of all believers. A democratic form of church government was restored by founders of Congregationalism who had
Puritan background. Numbers of other gospel truths were ignited
by the Spirit's flame through various religious groups. The table
of bread in the spiritual house was also restored. Divine healing,
feet washing, stewardship, immortality, and other vital doctrines
of the Scriptures came to light. Great was the day of reformation
when many Christian assemblies added their contribution to
reestablish apostolic Christianity.

The restoration of the proclamation demanding holiness is
of vital importance. God used John and Charles Wesley along
with George Whitefield as spiritual instruments in His hands to
erect the golden altar of sanctification. These men were expelled
from the Church of England because they proclaimed that no
person could be saved without holiness. Their followers were
first called "The Holy Club." Because of their order and system
by rule and method they later earned the name, "Methodists."
This vital contribution of the truth concerning holiness stirred a
great revival that awakened multitudes from their spiritual sleep
and death.

Attention is now drawn to the temple veil between the holy
place and the holy of holies. Remembering that it signifies the
broken body of our Lord, we readily understand how Christ in-
serted this truth in His temple. We gain entrance to the Father's
throne only through Christ's broken body. We are not saved by
observing creeds or doctrines. Church membership does not
grant entrance to God. Only as we are members of His body, the
church, do we answer Christ's prayer, "That they all may be one;
as thou, Father, art in me, and I in thee, that they also may be one
in us: that the world may believe that thou hast sent me" (John
17:21). Blessed was the day when this truth of unity in the body
of Christ was proclaimed. In the same manner as justification is
by faith, and sanctification and healing come by faith, church
membership is also by faith. Christ admits every blood-washed
soul into His body. By the same token, every sinner is excluded

regardless of his affiliation with religious sects. By Christ's stripes we are healed; by His poverty we become rich; by His death we receive life; by the torn temple veil which is His flesh, we become one body in the Spirit.

The last furnishing of the temple to be restored was the ark of the covenant. God's own law, the Holy Scripture, must be restored as the only creed and discipline of authority. The Shekinah of the Spirit's witness must be revealed in Christ's temple. Both God's mercy and justice must be proclaimed. The contemporary world has far outbalanced the mercy of God and rejected His justice. Christ himself must be exalted as our "mercy seat." Through Him we find expiation for sins. He is acclaimed Head of the church. The Church of God movement has dedicated its energies, strength, and spiritual power to make this contribution of truth to world Christianity. In the year 1880, D. S. Warner and other loyal saints banded together to restore this truth of unity of believers; the Holy Spirit, the sole Organizer of the church; the Word, Holy Scripture, the sole discipline of doctrine; Christ alone, Head of the church.

This is the temple the spiritual Jews (Christians) rebuild. Recently an appeal was made to a large religious assembly in America, requesting funds to erect an elaborate temple for Christ in Jerusalem. The man making the petition claimed to be one of the tourist guides, a keeper of the area in Jerusalem marked as the tomb of Jesus. He was a Jew who believed Jesus would come and reign in Jerusalem, and felt that he was responsible to have the throne of David ready for Him. He pointed to the prophecy in Zechariah to confirm the fact that Christ would come to Mount Olivet. This man is only one of a multitude who seem to be ignorant of the fact that Christ came to Mount Olivet almost two thousand years ago, fulfilling this prophecy. The angel Gabriel announced to Mary concerning the birth of Jesus as a child, "He shall be great and shall be called the Son of the Highest; and the Lord God shall give unto him the throne of his father David; and he shall reign over the house of Jacob forever; and of his kingdom there shall be no end" (Luke 1:32-33). All this reached spiritual fulfillment at Christ's first advent. While many are deceived into believing literal Jews will return to Jerusalem and reconstruct a literal temple where Christ will reign, true saints who understand will loyally toil in reconstructing the spiritual temple—the only structure Christ ever erected. Spiritual eyes are opened to see the same vision of truth acclaimed by the author of the Epistle to the Hebrews saying, "But ye are come unto mount Zion, and unto the city of the living God, the heavenly Jerusalem, and to an innumerable company of angels, To the general assembly and church of the firstborn, which are written in heaven" (Heb. 12:22-23a). In this our day Christ's temple is rebuilt and cleansed. The church is today the "habitation of God, through the Spirit."

The Witnesses Are Slain and Resurrected (Rev. 11:7-12)

It is common in apocalyptic literature for the author to introduce a theme, convey a number of events in chronological order, then revert back to the introductory thought. The subject is expressed again in more vivid symbols before the climax of the theme is reached. Chapter eleven of the Revelation is an example of this method used by John.

John is like an expert guide in an art gallery, lecturing to his students about a vast mural. First he has them stand back to absorb a general impression. The scope covers the prophecies of God to His people over centuries. He then draws the scholars closer to study details.

This chapter begins with John's vision of the church as a spiritual temple being measured. He then notes the temple being trodden under foot while the two witnesses, the Spirit and the Word, prophesy in sackcloth and ashes. At verse seven he reverts back to the introduction of the theme. Chronologically he begins with the testimony of the Spirit and the Word at the beginning of the Christian era. The Spirit made bold testimony beginning at Pentecost. Christ, the Living Word, vividly witnessed to the truth of God's spiritual temple. Later the written Word, the New Testament, gave powerful witness of the true church. This powerful witness then began to diminish with the rise of the apostasy which was evident even before the completion of the New Testament writings. John explains it this way: "And when they shall have finished their testimony, the beast that ascendeth out of the bottomless pit shall make war against them, and shall overcome them, and kill them" (Rev. 11:7). Here is a prophecy of the beast of Catholicism arising during the period of Dark Ages and charged with slaying the Spirit and the Word.

The papacy usurped human authority to govern the church. The pope of Rome exalted himself as the head of the religious body. The Holy Spirit is thus symbolized as being dead. Death means separation; truly the Holy Spirit was separated from the unclean works of the hierarchy of Rome. The Spirit's wisdom, life, and guidance was no more recognized by the system of the papacy than the authority of a dead man is respected. When the written Word was ignored and the laws of the Roman church became supreme, the power of the Scriptures is also symbolized as being dead. With the seating of the pontiff as head of the church, Christ the Word is in no way attached to the body of Romanism. As Rome thus made war against the Spirit and the Word, gradually the power of these two witnesses succumbed in their midst. John describes the horrid scene saying, "And their dead bodies shall lie in the street of the great city, which spiritually is called Sodom and Egypt, where also our Lord was crucified" (Rev. 11:8). Sodom stands for wickedness and immorality. This is always the inevitable result where the Spirit and Word are slain, and certainly depicts the conditions of the apostate world. Indeed, the wickedness and immorality of the religious body of Catholicism during the Dark Ages are appalling! Egypt is a symbol of bondage; just as literal Egypt held the ancient Jews in captivity, Roman Catholicism held true Christians in bondage. The masses were not only in bondage to Rome but in sinful bondage as well. There is no power in a religious organization where the Spirit and Word are dead, whereby a man may be saved from his sins. "Where our Lord was crucified" refers to Jerusalem where Christ was rejected as the only mediator and supreme ruler of the kingdom. With the rise of the papacy there were many mediators, and the pope claimed supreme power of the religious body; thus the true body of Christ is symbolized as being crucified.

It is important to note the bodies of the Spirit and the Word were not permitted burial. Rome endeavored to bury the Scriptures many times but God preserved them in a miraculous manner. Rome's efforts to bury the Spirit-governed church in martyrs' blood also failed. No earthly power can bury the Spirit of God! There is irony in the fact that even Rome itself claimed the forms of the Spirit and Word, yet denied their life and power. Paul wrote concerning "Traitors, heady, highminded, lovers of pleasure more than lovers of God; having a form of godliness, but denying the power thereof: from such turn away" (2 Tim. 3:4-5).

We note that the church, the spiritual body of Christ, was subjected to the same experiences as the physical body of our Lord. The true church was rejected, despised and crucified. Even as our Lord was lifted on the cross early in the morning, the early morning church of the gospel day was destined to suffer. On the day Christ died, when the sun should have been shining the brightest at the noon hour, the sun was eclipsed. In like manner during the gospel day when the light should have reached its zenith, there was an eclipse of the Sun of Righteousness, and the Dark Ages reigned. Physically Christ died at three o'clock in the afternoon. Spiritually, late in the afternoon of the gospel day, the apostasy reached its fullness, and the Spirit and the Word are symbolized as slain and powerless. In the beginning of this vision John first gives assurance to the true saints that the Spirit and Word will always be life and light to them, even though their prophecy was in sackcloth and ashes. Then he expresses that "in the street of the city" (Romanism, spiritual Babylon) the Spirit and Word are dead to those who choose to spiritually die and walk in darkness. This is an ever present truth.

Just as death could not hold the body of our Lord physically, neither could the Spirit and the Word be held in death's domain. The prophecy stated that they would lie in the street for three and one-half days. Prophetically, a day being equal to one year, this would mean three and one-half years. This makes the time period of the apostasy the same as the forty-two months—time, times and a dividing of time; or the same as one thousand, two hundred and three score days.[1] This is another way for the prophecy to predict the preservation and deliverance of the true body of Christ. Divine fulfillment of this prophecy terminated when the mighty Reformation of the sixteenth century was ushered in by the resurrection of the Spirit and the Word.

The physical resurrection of Christ is the keystone of the Christian faith. The spiritual resurrection of the Spirit and the Word is also imperative. When great reformers, set aflame with Holy Spirit power, declared truth at the peril of their lives, Rome's walls of bondage burst like a tomb in an earthquake. The Word, which had long been chained to the priests' pulpits and confined to the Latin language, became alive as it was placed in the hands of the people, in the common tongue. O glorious day of the blessed Reformation! Rome's tyranny was conquered. The gospel was again preached to the poor. Prisoners were loosed and sin's chains were broken. True life and light were again proclaimed.

The glory of the Reformation, however, has tarnished. Systems of the Protestant body have perpetuated some of the errors of Rome which killed the power of the two witnesses. Too often the Spirit is ignored as Administrator and Organizer of the church. Is it not tragically true that in many places the religious body is spiritually impotent? It is written concerning Christ, "He was in the world, and the world was made by him, and the world knew him not" (John 1:10). Could we likewise express the same

---

[1]See Time Table, p. 58.

blindness regarding the Spirit, saying, "The Spirit was in the church, and the church was made by him, and the church knew him not"? How beautiful is the truth that the same Holy Spirit which conceived the physical body of our Lord also conceives His spiritual body, the church. A divine church cannot be governed by human ingenuity. Energy of the flesh can run bazaars, organize social clubs and amusements, or raise millions; but only the Holy Spirit makes a temple for the Living God. Since the day of creation the Holy Spirit, who breathed upon the face of the deep and brought order out of chaos, longs to breathe upon the souls of men and again bring order, peace, and unity out of our chaotic world. The Spirit must not be ignored and cause human forms of worship to be cherished.

Under the cloak of Protestantism there is a malignant evil also oppressing the voice of the Word. Some deny that the Scriptures are divinely inspired. To others, anything supernatural in religion is discredited. The miracles, the Virgin Birth, experimental salvation, holiness, and divine healing have all been ridiculed. The divinity of our Lord, the Living Word, is frequently questioned. Sanctification is scoffed and immortality is believed to be a myth. When religious manuals are chosen to govern the spiritual body of the church rather than the New Testament, the Word is again rendered as powerless or dead, just as the laws of the Roman organization robbed the authority of the Word with their human laws.

The church must challenge today's Christians to express the same consecration as the early reformers. We need a new birth of the Spirit and a revival of preaching and practicing the Word. This is not the day for tolerance but for truth. Now is not the hour for peaceful coexistence with all the creeds and religions of men; rather it is the hour to proclaim war with all the counterfeit teachings of men. It is a day for positive action in the church to march forward with a bloodstained banner of the cross, a mighty sword of the Spirit, the power of the Living Word, and in the love of Jesus Christ.

Because the Spirit and the Word have been resurrected, there is a body of saints proclaiming that the **Spirit** alone is the sole organizer of the church. He gives spiritual gifts. Charismatic government is not optional for the Body of Christ—it is imperative. The **Word**, Christ, is restored as the only Head of the church. "And he is the head of the body, the church: who is the beginning, the firstborn from the dead; that in all things he might have preeminence" (Col. 1:18). Councils and committees, cardinals and bishops may elect a pope as the head of Romanism and Bishops to head the Protestant body; but God in heaven elected His Son, Jesus Christ, as the Head of the church.

This theme concludes with the Spirit and Word ascending into heaven. The allusion to Christ's ascension is evident. His body, the church, shall also ascend to the heavenly city. When Jesus said, "Heaven and earth shall pass away, but my words shall not pass away" (Matt. 24:35), He revealed the fact that our earthly world, sea and sky will be consumed and vanish away—but the Word is eternal. This old earth will be torn away and burned as a scaffold is removed when a building is completed. The spiritual structure of the church will be transported to the New Jerusalem. Paul's words shall come to pass: "Then cometh the end, when he shall have delivered up the kingdom to God, even the Father; when he shall have put down all rule and all authority and power. For he must reign, till he hath put all enemies under his feet. The last enemy that shall be destroyed is death" (I Cor. 15:24-26). Not only shall the living Word abide for all eternity, but also the Spirit shall dwell with the saints forever. Some have taught that there would be a day when the Holy Spirit would be withdrawn from the world before the end of time; but Jesus said, "And I will pray the Father, and he shall give you another Comforter, that he may abide with you for ever" (John 14:16). With spirit's wings the temple of Christ shall ascend through the skies to forever be the habitation of God through the Spirit. This is the temple which Christ builds.

The literal political nation of Israel, and a number of Christians believe Jesus will return to Jerusalem and establish a materialistic kingdom. Plans are already designed for Christ's temple. Money has been sent to Jerusalem for this purpose. There are four major problems:

1. The Mosque of Omar, a Moslem Temple, is erected on the exact site where Solomon's Temple was built. Jews believe this Mosaic structure must be destroyed to build the temple for Messiah.
2. There is no pure-blooded descendant of Aaron who can be found to serve as High Priest.
3. It is repulsive to the Jews to restore animal sacrifices.
4. The Palestinian Arabs possess the land desired by Jews.

The Bible proclaims, "As you come to him, the living Stone —rejected by men but chosen by God and precious to him—you also, like living stones, are being built into a spiritual house to be a holy priesthood, offering spiritual sacrifices acceptable to God through Jesus Christ" (I Peter 2:4, 5 NIV.) The only High Priest is Jesus. To offer blood sacrifices is to blaspheme the blood of Jesus, "because it is impossible for the blood of bulls and goats to take away sins" (Hebrews 10:4 NIV). Jesus established His kingdom at His first advent. When He comes again He will deliver up the kingdom. The Apostle Paul wrote, "For as in Adam all die, so in Christ all will be made alive. But each in his own turn: Christ, the firstfruits; then, when he comes, those who belong to him. Then the end will come, when he hands over the kingdom to God the Father after he has destroyed all dominion, authority and power. For he must reign until he has put all his enemies under his feet. The last enemy to be destroyed is death" (I Corinthians 15:22-26 NIV).

God's Chosen Nation

"Blessed is the nation whose God is the Lord; and the people whom he hath chosen for his own inheritance. The Lord looketh from heaven; he beholdeth all the sons of men" (Psalm 33:12, 13). The "nation whose God is the Lord"—what nation is that? We would all like to believe that America is that nation. However, other world nations are not convinced our God is the Lord. Russia in competition with us is convinced our god is "Science." China, seeing America armed to the hilt as a colossal giant, concludes our god is "War." India's starving millions with envy note our abundance of food and weight reducing emphasis and believe America's god is her "Belly." Japan, following the American pattern, would deduce our god is "Production." Africa, remembering our racial problems, concludes our god is "Racial Pride." Europe may come a little nearer to the truth with the opinion our god is the "Dollar." To see America's advertisements one would get the impression America's god is "Sex," "Sensuality," or "Security." In spite of all these negative concepts we do believe America to be the most righteous nation in the world. God has abundantly blessed us! To the measure we have been righteous we have been exalted. "Righteousness exalteth a nation but sin is a reproach to any people" (Proverbs 14:34). It must be noted, however, that America is not the nation referred to in the book of Psalms.

Many people believe Israel as a political nation, now established as a world power, to be God's chosen nation. The victory of Israel in the six-day war with Egypt is pointed to with reference as evidence that God has made the Jews a people of special privilege. It seems many religious folk forget some New Testament passages of scripture. In Acts 10:34-35 it is written, "Then Peter opened his mouth and said, Of a truth I perceive that God is no respecter of persons; but in every nation he that feareth him, and worketh righteousness, is accepted with him." The apostle Paul declares, "There is neither Jew nor Greek, there is neither bond nor free, there is neither male nor female; for ye are all one in Christ Jesus. And if ye be Christ's, then are ye Abraham's seed, and heirs according to the promise" (Galatians 3:28).

God's chosen nation is not defined by physical birth or political position. Not all Jews by birth were Abraham's seed. It must be noted that Abraham gave birth to both Ishmael and Isaac, but God chose only Isaac for the inheritance. The descendants of Ishmael are now the Arab people at war with Israel. Isaac was the father of Jacob and Esau, but God chose Jacob for the inheritance. Some Jews of Jesus' day claimed to be Abraham's seed, but Jesus challenged their claim (John 8:39-45). Through all generations God's election for His chosen people was predicated upon a demand of being children of God by faith. The Israel of the Old Testament prophetically portrays the church as God's chosen nation. Isaiah writes, "Who hath heard such a thing? Who hath seen such things? Shall the earth be made to bring forth in a day? Or shall a nation be born at once? For as soon as Zion travailed she brought forth her children" (Isaiah 66:8). This nation, chosen of God, was born on the Day of Pentecost. Peter describes this chosen nation very beautifully as a nation of holy people. "But ye are a chosen people, a royal priesthood, a holy nation, a people belonging to God, that you may declare the praises of him who called you out of darkness into his wonderful light. Once you were not a people, but now you are the people of God; once you had not received mercy, but now you have received mercy." (I Peter 2:9, 10).

The citizens of the new nation chosen of God are described as spiritual Jews. Paul writes to the Christians in Rome saying, "For he is not a Jew, which is one outwardly; neither is that circumcision which is outwardly in the flesh. But he is a Jew, which is one inwardly; and circumcision is that of the heart, in the spirit" (Romans 2:28, 29a).

New Testament prophecies of God's provision, protection, and promise of inheritance are given for His chosen nation, the church. Our citizenship is by a new birth. The seal of Heaven's commonwealth is the circumcision of the heart by the Holy Spirit. True Christians by faith are the King's people and heirs of His promise. "The Spirit itself beareth witness with our spirit, that we are the children of God: and if children, then heirs; heirs of God, and joint-heirs with Christ" (Romans 8:16-17).

There is much talk today about Jews going back to Jerusalem literally. It must be noted that all of Palestine is only about one-fourth the size of the State of Indiana. The truth is very vivid when understood. Like the ancient Jews returned to their true worship, restoring the temple at Jerusalem before the first advent of the Messiah, the church is being restored in these last days before the Second Advent of our Lord. God's chosen Nation, the church, was scattered, divided, and persecuted during the days of the apostasy while Romanism ruled like ancient Babylon. At the birth of the Reformation, Christians began to return to the mountain of truth. In Hebrews it is described, "But ye are come unto Mount Zion, and unto the city of the living God, the heavenly Jerusalem . . ." (Hebrews 10:22). The church is the true temple of our Lord. This is the chosen nation!

The inheritance is His kingdom, "Hath not God chosen the poor of this world rich in faith, and heirs of the kingdom which he hath promised to them that love him?" (James 2:5). Our inheritance is not earthly goods nor political power, not even a millennium of peace. Peter said, "To an inheritance incorruptible and undefiled, and that fadeth not away, reserved in heaven for you, who are kept by the power of God through faith unto salvation ready to be revealed in the last time" (I Peter 1:4-5.) Peter made sure of his reservation in the Holy City, have you?

CHAPTER V

MYSTERY BABYLON
(Revelation, Chapter 17)

Better houses but not improved homes; greater wealth but less happiness; wonder drugs but not better health; accelerating speed but lack of direction; increased knowledge but less wisdom; more churches but fewer saints; this is the chaotic picture of today's world. It looks like a crazy quilt with many patches but no design. Paradoxical as it may sound, civilization is making progress in reverse!

Confusion and chaos are the results of man's ignoring God. God alone knows the pattern for the world created by His hand. When man excludes God from his plans, it is as disastrous as flying a plane with only one wing. Until we learn that the wing of materialism must have a balance-wing of spiritual strength, we shall continue going in circles and heading for calamity. This is true politically, socially, scientifically, economically, and most of all, religiously. The Bible has the answer for our mixed-up world.

Babylon Means Confusion

Humanity is ever the same; man's foolish pride always tempts him to willfully disregard God. Even the flood which destroyed the antediluvian world could not erase this characteristic from man's carnal nature. It was Nimrod, the great-grandson of Noah, who planned to outwit God by building a waterproof tower reaching to the sky—a place of security in the event that there would be another flood. This is evidence that Nimrod did not believe the rainbow promise. He also defied God to destroy the human race. However, God has a way of humbling proud men who endeavor to build their own way to heaven. He thwarted Nimrod's foolish scheme by causing a diversity of languages among the tower builders. Unity of counsel and action became impossible, and fostered mistrust and misunderstanding. The unfinished tower was named "Babel," which means confusion. The city where the tower stood later came to be known as Babylon, and is connected with Bab-ilu, interpreted as "the gate of God."

Babylon Means Bondage

Centuries after its origin, Babylon again comes to view as the mighty empire of Nebuchadnezzar. This capital city was fifteen miles square and was situated in the Euphrates-Tigris Valley, on the site where it is believed the Garden of Eden was located. The city was divided by the Euphrates River at its center. Large bricks cemented together with bitumen formed the massive city walls. Twenty-five gates of brass on each side of the city were well protected by two hundred and fifty observation towers. The Babylonians were confident that their city was impregnable.

As might be expected by its measure of wealth and outward splendor, Babylon was the seat of boundless luxury, and the home of a people addicted to self-indulgence. Money broke many ties; wine and women contributed to immorality; even religious worship was defiled with sacred prostitution. Once in her lifetime, every woman had to visit the temple of Belus and fall into the embrace of any stranger who would throw a piece of gold into her lap.

During the reign of Nebuchadnezzar, the Israelites were captured and brought as slaves into wicked Babylon. Songs of Zion were silenced and offerings for Israel's sins could no longer be made at Jerusalem's pillaged temple. The children of Israel were often beaten, persecuted, and despised during their captivity. Many of them became like their heathen neighbors; but God preserved a remnant who never bowed to idols. At the fulfillment of Daniel's prophecy, the seventy years' captivity ended, and Nehemiah and Ezra were granted permission to lead the exiled Jews back to Jerusalem to rebuild the city. Astonishing as it may seem, a number of Jews preferred to remain as slaves to Babel's lords, rather than to endure the hardships of returning to Jerusalem where freedom would be enjoyed. Some Jews who chose to stay in Babylon reasoned that all their possessions were there; others had married into Babylonian families; a few had even attained positions of prominence. Therefore, they chose to die in Babylon.

Literal Babylon Fell

Jeremiah, the prophet, foretold the utter destruction of ancient Babylon. The decline of the mighty empire began when it fell into the hands of the Medes and Persians. In the year 500 B.C. Darius Hystaspis ordered the walls and gates to be destroyed, and the people evicted from their homes. Later, King Zerxes (probably the Ahasuerus of the Bible) plundered the temple and carried away the golden image of Belus. Nearly two hundred years later when Alexander the Great conquered the city, he employed ten thousand men to work for two months clearing away the debris. Since the days of Alexander four capitals have been built from the remains of the golden empire. The great city, the beauty of the Chaldees, has thus emphatically "become heaps" (Jer. 51:37). She is truly "an astonishment, and a hissing, without an inhabitant" (Jer. 51:37). Her walls have altogether disappeared; they have fallen (Jer. 51:44). Her land has become a wilderness; wild beasts of the desert lie there and owls dwell therein. The natives regard the whole site haunted, and neither will the Arabs pitch tent nor shepherds fold sheep there.[1] The great city which had been exalted to the skies, so to speak, was laid even with the dust.

Mystic Babylon

(See Picture Chart following page 32: Strip 4)

The Old Testament records the story of King Ahab and Jezebel (I Kings 16:31). Ahab, King of Israel, married Jezebel, a

---

[1]*Smith's Bible Dictionary.*

pagan who worshiped idols. She brought her heathen religion and pagan gods with her into Israel. She killed the true prophets of God and fed the prophets of Baal. Elijah fled to the wilderness to save his life. God fed and protected him there for three and one half years. This is the background for Mystic Babylon.

John the Revelator describes his vision of a woman who displays upon her forehead the name, "Mystery, Babylon the Great, the Mother of Harlots and Abomination of the Earth." John is carried away into a wilderness and sees this woman clothed in scarlet and purple, decked with gold, precious stones and pearls, having a golden cup in her hand which is full of her abominations and filthiness of her fornication. The wicked woman rides a scarlet-colored beast full of names of blasphemy, having seven heads and ten horns. She is also pictured as sitting upon many waters and is not only a harlot but a drunken one, intoxicated with the blood of martyrs.

With such a vision, it is no wonder John shook in amazement. The combination of symbols includes creatures from the animal and human category. According to our "key" this signifies a political-religious power. A scarlet beast with seven heads and ten horns is familiar since it was described in Revelation, chapter twelve. In the seventeenth chapter, John inquired of the angel concerning these seven heads. The angel explained that the heads were seven kings—five had already fallen in John's day; the sixth, the Imperial, was the ruling form of government at the time of the Revelation to John; and there was one more to follow. All this is fulfilled in Rome, a beastly empire which persecuted Christians as ancient Babylon had persecuted the Jews. This scarlet beast is depicted in both its pagan and papal forms. Literal Babylon historically was also designated in two forms: the Chaldo-Assyrian city and the later empire.

This harlot woman John saw in the wilderness is drawn in sharp contrast to the holy pristine woman in chapter twelve of Revelation, who is seen in the glories of all heavenly light. The symbolism is evident that as the pure sun-clothed woman represented the true mother church, this mother of harlots stands for an apostate religious body in the wilderness of sin. Here is a vivid description of paganism (mystery, Babylon the great), papalism (mother of harlots), and sectarianism (abominations of the earth). Like ancient Babylon, she claims to be "the gate God." Her attire is gold, precious stones and pearls. How different from the woman standing on the moon clothed with the sun! One woman is heavenly, the other is worldly. The apostate woman is described as a harlot because she is married to the kings of the earth. The union between the Roman Catholic church and world sovereigns throughout history is really astounding. During the Dark Ages when Roman Catholicism was supreme, the power it exerted controlled great monarch leaders. A well-known example is given in the case of Pope Gregory VII and Henry IV of Germany. The pope attempted to make reforms but Henry refused to recognize these innovations. The pope excommunicated the emperor and robbed him of his kingdom. The result was that Henry was forced to seek pardon. He found the pontiff at Conossa, but was not granted an audience until he stood for four days barefooted in the snow of the palace courtyard. Many other records verify the power of popes to rule civil kingdoms.

This harlot woman is not intoxicated alone with red wine that sparkles in a cup, but with the blood of the saints she has slain as martyrs. The figurative speech is an allusion to a cup of drugged wine with which lewd women inflamed the passions of their lovers. Jeremiah, the prophet, used the same metaphor in describing the Chaldean Babylon saying, "The nations have drunken of her wine; therefore the nations are mad" (Jer. 51:7b). Ancient Babylon's persecution, slavery and killing of the Jews were but a mere shadow-picture of the horrid fulfillment by mystery Babylon. Martyrs of the Dark Ages were stabbed, stoned, shot, drowned, hanged, beheaded, burned, baked in ovens, sunken in the mire, starved, and frozen. Others suffered death by being cast from towers, stuffed and blown up with gunpowder, ripped with swords, bored with hot irons, hacked with axes, and torn piecemeal by red-hot pinchers. By the cruel claws of the scarlet beast, others were tied to horses' tails and dragged through the streets, or choked to death with water, lime, rags, mangled pieces of their own bodies, or urine. It would be difficult to invent any new means of torture or death. The bloodthirsty beast is also guilty of killing so-called heretics by scalping them, trampling them until the bowels are forced out, tying their intestines to trees and pulling them forth by degrees, feeding them to wild beasts, twisting their heads off, cutting them up in small pieces, or butchering them like sheep.

When Roman priests are questioned today concerning these things, they claim this was done by the civil powers, not the popes. This is true only in the measure that the deeds were carried out by civil powers, which were completely controlled by the pope. It is depicted in the vision John saw as a woman riding and controlling the beast. This authority was so widely spread that it is symbolized as the woman sitting upon many waters. Water is used to signify people, such as we often say, "a great sea of faces."

"Abomination of the earth" is an expression used to describe the corruption of the apostate church through the ages and even until the end of time. In Paul's day this apostate church was only in the embryo stage. Yet he describes her as "the mystery of iniquity" (2 Thess. 2:7), which was already at work. The iniquity has increased until there can scarcely be named any crime or transgression which has not been committed by the church of Rome. In this religion it is lawful to steal, lie, cheat, kill, or use any means, good or bad, if it will result in final gain for the church; the end justifies the means. The purple attire of the Roman church is spotted even to the undergarments with the filth of avarice. Her jewels of adornment were purchased at the cost of making merchandise of the souls of men. Her hands are repeatedly filled with money to purchase pardon for souls in purgatory; she is guilty of fraud. In sharp contrast with the star-crowned woman whose diadem was the glory of the apostles of the Lamb, the unchaste woman rides a scarlet beast which has the names of blasphemy upon its heads. She is known to the world as one who claims power to save or damn, to be infallible and to exert authority as the vicar of the Son of God. (Two popes. have claimed the position as head of the church at the same time.) To her sin of blasphemy the sin of immorality is added. Though the scarlet garments of Rome were wide and long, they could not keep hidden the licentious deeds of her popes. Some of them lived in open infamy, with prostitutes bearing their children. The heart of Rome is filled with murders for which she has never repented. Yet, with all her sins she boasts of her "holy apostolic succession." The corruption of ancient Babylon is repeated in "king size" under the name of mystery Babylon, the mother of harlots, abominations of the earth.

The Mother of Harlots

The comparison of the two women depicted in the Revelation continues with the fact that both of them are mothers. The holy church gave birth to one body, the man-child, but the apostate woman gave birth to many daughters. The offspring is always of the same nature, flesh, blood, and spirit as the parents. When the New Testament church gave birth to a body of Christians constituting "one new man" in Christ (Eph. 2:15), it produced more of itself. In like manner the daughters of the apostate church are her offspring, and project the very nature, system and spirit of their mother. This is a terrible indictment against Protestant bodies born out of the Roman Catholic church. It must be quickly stated that not all persons in divided Protestantism are infected with the gross evils of the Roman mother. It is the systems of Romanism which have been inbred in Protestant bodies that continue to generate her nature.

The Protestant daughters of Roman Catholicism were as innocent at birth as a little child is innocent, even though it may be born of illegitimate parents. The older these religious bodies become, the more they befit the nature of their mother. Some of them honor her with deep veneration, calling her "Our Holy Mother Church"; but God has named her "mother of harlots, abomination of the earth."

An early trait of the Roman Catholic church became evident when her oldest daughters were born. They carried into Protestantism the state church. It is a historical fact that Luther gave to Germany a state church; Henry VIII founded the Established Church of England as a state religion; John Knox carried to Scotland the combined powers of church and state; Zwingli fought with a sword in one hand and the Bible in the other to establish the state religion of Protestantism in Switzerland. When Protestant sects first became established and had power in their hands, they acted much in the same manner as the church of Rome before them, imprisoning, banishing, persecuting, and even putting to death those who opposed them. Protestant bodies not only fought the Catholics but other Protestants as well. You will recall it was the persecution of the Protestant Church of England that forced Puritans and Pilgrims to American shores.

In the physical family the children inherit human traits and features of their parents. In like manner, spiritually speaking, the daughters of mother Babylon bear her image, nature, and various distinguished traits. Some believe in transubstantiation (the bread and wine of communion become the actual flesh and blood of Christ); others baptize their infants or maintain sprinkling as a mode of baptism; some maintain the system of joining the church through the minister and of observing certain rituals originating with Mother Babylon rather than with the New Testament church. Assuming the right to form church creeds and disciplines and to name their religious bodies are also likenesses to the Roman mother. A religion of good works to attain salvation is very much at home with many Protestant groups, and roots in Roman Catholicism. Romanism makes room for a chance of salvation after death; some of her daughters do likewise with a millennial teaching.

The daughters are also charged with doctrines of devils. To Protestantism's shame there are some teachings under her religious blanket that excel the errors of Rome. The denial of Christ's divinity, the divine inspiration of the Scriptures, the rejection of the Atonement, the discarding of the miracles and all the supernatural power of the Christian faith, and the disbelief of immortality, of heaven and hell are devilish doctrines which were never taught by the Roman Catholic church. No wonder John said that the true worshippers on Mount Zion "were not defiled with women; for they are virgins" (Rev. 14:4). True saints of God are virgins—not married to these harlot daughters of the Roman Catholic church.

Babylon Is Fallen (Rev. Chapter 18)

Just as Jerusalem is a term used to signify the New Testament church as a mother and is also used as the name for the city of God's dwelling place, Babylon is the term used to designate the apostate mother church and also refers to the city which is the stronghold of Satan. The supremacy of the Roman Catholic church was destined to cease. The ten kingdoms of the empire opposed her and cast her aside, as an old wrinkled, haggard prostitute is cast off by her lovers.

Like Nimrod, Catholicism planned a tower of works to reach to the sky, making its own way to heaven. But a confusion of spiritual languages divided the builders who now have scattered into different directions. Each sect speaks its own spiritual tongue and formulates its own interpretation of the Scriptures. Babylon in her pagan, papal, and Protestant forms combines into a trinity of confusion; inside her walls many of God's children are held in bondage.

Rome's temporal power was first to fall. The great sovereign empire of the world was reduced to a tiny state of only 110 acres; it could fit seven times over in New York's Central Park. During the days of the sixteenth-century Reformation, the spiritual walls of mystery Babylon began to shake and crumble.

Out of her remains, a number of other cities of confusion were constructed in a Protestant world. Great reformers opened Babylon's gates urging true saints to return to spiritual Jerusalem and restore the temple of God. However, many became lost in a wilderness of confusion with sectarian creeds to shackle them. The prophecies foretell such a cloudy day as this:

> ". . . I (John) saw another angel come down from heaven, having great power; . . . And he cried mightily with a strong voice, saying, Babylon the great is fallen, is fallen, and is become the habitation of devils, and the hold of every foul spirit, and a cage of every unclean and hateful bird. For all nations have drunk of the wine of the wrath of her fornication, and the kings of the earth have committed fornication with her, and the merchants of the earth are waxed rich through the abundance of her delicacies. And I heard another voice from heaven, saying, Come out of her, my people, that ye be not partakers of her sins, and that ye receive not of her plagues. For her sins have reached unto heaven, and God hath remembered her iniquities." (Rev. 18:1-5).

Today true prophets sound this warning over Babel's courts. It is with grief that we hear some say they will not return to restore the New Testament church in spiritual Zion. They give the same excuses literal Jews gave long ago when Nehemiah called for exiled Jews to restore Jerusalem. Some say their spiritual possessions still remain in Babylon; others have been married or united with churches who are Babylon's daughters; some hold places of prominence in Babel's courts and are in bondage to her lords. The result will be that they shall die in Babylon.

Inside Babylon's broken walls, creeping devils of strange religious cults make their abode. Lurking at almost every door the anti-Christian doctrine of Jehovah's Witnesses with the denial of Christ's divinity and rejection of the trinity. Their "no hell" doctrine has forced its poisonous venom into the multitudes. Like an unclean bird, the errors of Christian Science have plucked the eyes of thousands of souls, blinding them to truth.

Mary Baker Eddy's statement that there is no more power in the blood of Christ than is contained in the blood of her veins is a lie from the pit. To teach her followers that they should address their prayers to her as "Mother" and pray, "Our Father-Mother God," is utter blasphemy! The whole world should know that Mrs. Eddy was once a spiritualist medium.[2]

When the Mormon choir sings the Christmas carols over radio and television it is difficult to believe that they deny the virgin birth. The foul spirit they harbor in their belief concerning polygamy should be sufficient to warn any honest soul from being misled into their doctrine. They teach that Christ was a polygamist; that Mary and Martha were his plural wives, and Mary Magdalene was another. They also claim that the wedding feast at Cana was for Christ's own wedding. Their doctrine maintains that men should have many wives to produce bodies for the souls being born through their great seers, such as Joseph Smith and Brigham Young who now are supposed to inhabit one of the planets. These are only a few examples of the unclean birds and foul spirits which now inhabit Babylon!

The Pure Bride of Christ Rev. 19)

After denouncing the "harlot woman," the prophecies present the beautiful true bride of Christ. She is composed of all the true saints who are "arrayed in fine linen, clean and white: for the fine linen is the righteousness of the saints" (Rev. 19:8). The relationship of Christ and the church is most beautifully portrayed using marriage as the figure of speech.

The "marriage of the Lamb" has become a common figure of speech. Paul, the Apostle, refers to it when writing the Ephesian letter, saying, "Husbands, love your wives, even as Christ also loved the church, and gave himself for it; that he might sanctify and cleanse it with the washing of water by the word, that he might present it to himself a glorious church, not having

---

[2]Van Baalen, Jan Karel, *Gist of the Cults*, p.36.

spot, or wrinkle, or any such thing; but that it should be holy and without blemish" (Eph. 5:25-27). The Lamb's wife prepares for her wedding, and her clean garments are free from all marks of the beast. The church is also clearly presented with the comparison of the two Adams. The first Adam (Adam means beginning) needed a helpmate. Therefore God caused a deep sleep to fall upon him, and removed a rib from his side which was used in forming woman. Christ, the last Adam, also had His side pierced, and from it came the blood which would form His bride. It is written, "Take heed therefore unto yourselves, and to all the flock, over the which the Holy Ghost hath made you overseers, to feed the church of God, which he hath purchased with his own blood" (Acts 20:28). The deep sleep of death fell upon the Christ while from His side the blood flowed. The hand of God gathered the blood and creatures of human clay, dust of the earth, and formed the church. The same Holy Spirit that breathed into the nostrils of clay so that Eve became a living soul, breathed into the spiritual bride of Christ as a mighty wind on the day of Pentecost, and the church became a living bride. For this reason Paul exclaims, "For we are members of his body, of his flesh, and of his bones" (Eph. 5:30). Since the day of creation when the "Spirit of God moved upon the face of the waters" (Gen. 1:2), bringing light out of darkness, separating the water from the land, and breathing life into mortal man, He has always maintained His office of bringing order out of chaos. On the day of Pentecost the Holy Spirit created unity of language, spirit, and purpose out of the confusion, strife, and divisions of men. The only power great enough to create order out of today's chaos is the Spirit of God. He alone can bring unity out of Babylon's divisions, creating one body, the bride of Christ.

With the symbol of a bride, holiness is acclaimed. Christ's bride is not being courted with the lords of Babylon. Neither is she flirting with the world. Sinful pleasures and lustful desires have no place in her heart for she is betrothed to a holy Bridegroom. She is beautifully clothed in the fine linen which is the righteousness of the saints. Her spirit is the Holy Spirit.

Many of God's children are lost in churches where truth is not taught. We must love them and pray for ways to share the message of true salvation and a holy life style.

Marriage vows include the commitment, forsaking all others, to love, honor, and obey. The union is to remain under all circumstances—for better or for worse, in sickness and in health, also in plenty or in want, even until death. The Christian is united with Christ under the same commitment. We, too, forsake all to be His disciples; we must love, honor, and obey Him. No matter what the circumstances of life may be, there is never any just cause for separation from Christ. Even death cannot sever this holy union; it is eternal. There are some who once were united with the Lord but today they are separated and divorced. A divorcement from Christ is gross sin. Yet, it is written, "Turn, O backsliding children, saith the Lord; for I am married unto you" (Jer. 3:14a).

The Old Testament story of Hosea reveals a husband who loved his wife, Gomer, even when she fell to the depths of sin. In the heart of Hosea there was an unquenchable flame of love. Gomer rejected her devoted companion, and stubborn rebellion led her into paths of lustful wickedness. She sold herself into sin which resulted in literal slavery. Hosea found Gomer in the slave market and bought her back—all because he loved her too much to let her go. This is a shadow of the unquenchable flame of love in Christ's heart for even those who divorce Him and return to the slave market of sin. He loves each soul too much to let it go. Therefore the blood was shed to pay the ransom price to buy again the backslider.

A bride willingly takes the family name of the bridegroom's father. Christ prayed for the church to be kept in His Father's name (John 17:11). John the Baptist clearly explained that he was not the bridegroom but the bridegroom's friend. John said, "He that hath the bride is the bridegroom: but the friend of the bridegroom, which standeth and heareth him, rejoiceth greatly because of the bridegroom's voice: this my joy therefore is fulfilled" (John 3:29). John the Baptist is a wonderful "best man" at the wedding, but the bride never takes the name of the "best man." Neither is any apostle or reformer the bridegroom; the marriage union is with Christ our Lord and the church. He alone has redeemed her with His precious blood.

During the days of slavery in the South a young Negro named Mose fell deeply in love with Julia, a slave on the neighboring plantation. Mose was a free slave who chose to remain with his master; he received small wages for his labor. Never did a day go by without Mose counting the coins he eagerly had saved to buy Julia's freedom. He was awakened early one morning with the noise of horses and stagecoaches traveling by his meager quarters to the adjoining farm. Seeing a cloud of dust as many more people passed by, he knew this meant there would be a public sale that day at this nearby estate. Even his dark skin grew a little pale with the thought that some slave merchant might buy Julia.

Mose reached for his bag of coins under the pillow and tied them about his neck, then hurriedly joined the crowd at the public sale. By the time the midday sun was high in the sky, the auctioneer had sold all the cattle to high bidders. Next for auction came the slaves. First a screaming little Negro child was pulled from his mother's hands and dangled by one arm as the auctioneer cried, "What am I bid for this kid? What am I bid?" The Negro mammy clutched the black boots of the auctioneer and begged "Oh, please, sah, donna sella my baby—please sah." The man replied with a kick from the black boot, and the little child was sold for a very paltry sum. (Dear God, forgive us for these sins of America.) Several other slaves were marketed, and then Mose saw that Julia was next upon the old tree stump used as the auction block. Treated like an animal, Julia was being auctioned as the auctioneer cried, "She weighs 120 pounds, is only seventeen years old, is a good worker and labors many hours in the field." He yanked her mouth open and told the number of teeth she had. Then even before he called for the bid Mose shouted, "I bids, sah, I bids." He opened the bag of coins and presented all the money he possessed. The crowd laughed and the auctioneer sneered as he kicked the coins around on the ground and angrily shouted, "Fool, who would sell a slave girl for such a worthless sum?"

The heart of Mose sank into despair when Julia was purchased by the merchant in a high silk hat who had already bought heavily at the auction. There was only one thing to do, Mose thought, and muttered under his breath, "I'll take her place!" It was evening when at last the wealthy merchant consented to exchange Julia for Mose, the free slave. Convinced that a male slave could render more labor, the merchant signed the legal statement, giving Julia freedom but making Mose a bondaged slave. The chief justice sealed the document and gave a copy to Julia, who placed it inside her dress near her heart.

The steamboat on the Mississippi River was being loaded with all the purchases of the rich man in the high silk hat and the captain called, "All Aboard!" Mose knew that this meant him and the other slaves from the market. He tightly clasped Julia's hand, pressed it to his lips, and softly whispered, "Be true to me, dear. I will return and you will be my bride."

With flowing tears streaming down her cheeks Julia faithfully promised, "Oh, Mose, I will, I will. I can never know why you are taking my place. If it were not for you I would be on board that boat going to be a slave on a new plantation. Why did you do it, Mose, why?"

"Because I love you," he replied as he joined the others to board the boat. The whistle blew and the steamer was soon out of sight. As long as Julia could see the silhouette of the boat against the sunset she waved good-bye to her lover.

A small shed furnished shelter for Julia to rest for the night. She was rudely awakened shortly after dawn by a firm hand and a commanding voice. Rubbing her eyes she thought it was a nightmare; but no—it was the merchant man who had purchased her the day before. He was trying to get the copy of her freedom papers. She leaped from her bed and hurriedly ran to the chief justice. The unjust merchant followed her and demanded that she be awarded to him.

"But her papers are in order, sir; you cannot touch her. She is free because a man has taken her place," explained the chief justice.

"But," argued the merchant, "last night the steamer went down in the storm. All that I purchased is lost, so I have come to reclaim this ugly slave."

Before any reply could be made, Julia, trembling and in tears cried, "You means, sah, my Mose is dead?" As fast as her legs could carry her she ran to the banks of the Mississippi and called over the muddy waves, "Oh, Mose, you died for me—you died for me."

I love this story because you see, I am Julia. It was not my skin but my heart that was black. From heaven's plantation Jesus saw me and came to save me from Satan, the merchant of souls; but all the silver and gold in the world could not redeem me. Life was the auctioneer, and when I became Satan's slave Jesus took my place to let me become free. He gave me a copy of the Bible which is signed with His blood and sealed by the Holy Spirit, the chief justice. When Satan comes to claim me I appeal to the Holy Spirit and open the Word; these both testify that I am free. Jesus has promised to return, and I am a part of His waiting bride. Often I run to Calvary and cry, "You died for me; how much You must love me!" Each day I press my robe of right-eousness and fill my lamp with oil, for we know not at what hour the Bridegroom cometh.

Mystery Babylon's Final Doom

"And the great city was divided into three parts, and the cities of the nation fell: the great Babylon came in remembrance before God, to give unto her the cup of the wine of the fierceness of his wrath" (Rev. 16:19). This prophecy will be fulfilled at the day of judgment. Babylon's trinity—paganism, papalism, and humanism—shall face the wrath and judgment of God. John further describes it saying, "And the light of a candle shall shine no more in thee; and the voice of the bridegroom and of the bride shall be heard no more at all in thee: for thy merchants were the great men of the earth; for by thy sorceries were all nations deceived. And in her was found the blood of prophets, and of saints, and of all that were slain upon the earth" (Rev. 18:23-24). The voice of God calls loudly today bidding true saints to flee from Babylon to Zion before her destruction comes. There is a thrill when one notes in the prophecies that sheep do hear the Shepherd's voice and come out.

Babylon's dragon, beast, and false prophet are last seen "cast into the lake of fire and brimstone," and are "tormented day and night for ever and ever" (Rev. 20:10). But while God's judgment is poured out upon Babylon, the true bride is enjoying the marriage feast in the Father's house. Like the Parable of the Prodigal Son, the story ends with the feast still continuing.

CHAPTER IV

THE REIGN OF CHRIST
(Revelation Chapter 20)

Have you ever heard of a "golden age" when all human dreams are to become a reality? It is to be a day when every man will sit under his own vine, enjoy his own fig tree, and live to beget a thousand children. This land of the Messianic age promises to produce a wheat straw which will grow to the size of a palm tree, and one grain of wheat which will make several sacks of flour. A single bunch of grapes will load a ship; even one grape will be large enough to make several kegs of wine. It is dreamed the animals will all be tame, snakes will not be poisonous, and every desert will blossom with roses. Sickness, poverty, sorrow, and pain will be vanquished, and women will no longer suffer in childbirth. Manna will again fall from heaven to feed the multitudes. Swords will all be beaten into plowshares and war will be unknown. Even the Devil is to be bound for one thousand years!

This was the dream of ancient Jews who eagerly anticipated a Messiah who would come and fulfill their fantasy. Scribes who copied the Old Testament Scriptures often included in their writings the oral law as well as the inspired word of God. The oral law imbibed the Jewish traditions which fostered a carnal hope of an earthly, materialistic kingdom. When the Messiah came, a spiritual kingdom was ushered in which "is not meat and drink; but righteousness, and peace, and joy in the Holy Ghost" (Rom. 14:17). Therefore, the Messiah was rejected. Jesus told the scribes and Pharisees that they were blinded by their traditions, saying, "Full well ye reject the commandment of God, that ye may keep your own tradition" (Mark 7:9). Again He uttered, "For had ye believed Moses, ye would have believed me: for he wrote of me. But if ye believe not his writings, how shall ye believe my words?" (John 5:46-47).

Repeatedly the New Testament notes that Christ fulfilled the prophecies of His first advent. Isaiah's expression concerning the animals being tame is figurative speech depicting the beastly natures of human beings. When Christ died to save humanity from the carnal nature, He provided the blood with power to make new creatures. Wild, ravenous, sin-spotted individuals became meek and gentle as lambs.

When the Water of Life flowed from the Messiah into the barren, sin-parched souls of men, they burst forth with the Rose of Sharon and the Lily of the Valley. Thus, the desert of the sinful soul blossoms like a rose.

The true saints, who are the "holy nation of God," gathered out from all nations and peoples, dwell in peace on Mount Zion. Their weapons of warfare are transformed into tools of righteousness. Isaiah's words, "They shall beat their swords into plowshares, and their spears into pruning hooks: nation shall not lift up sword against nation, neither shall they learn war anymore" (Isa. 2:4), were fulfilled in the Christ who came and brought, "Peace on earth, good will toward men."

Such pictures are not intended to describe temporal, political kingdoms of earth, but the happy state of God's holy nation of saints. Micah prophesies where this reign will be, saying, "And the Lord shall reign over them in Mount Zion from henceforth, even for ever" (Mic. 4:7). This is the spiritual Zion Paul speaks of in Hebrews 12:22-23: "But ye are come unto mount Sion, and unto the city of the living God, the heavenly Jerusalem, and to an innumerable company of angels, to the general assembly and church of the firstborn, which are written in heaven, and to God the Judge of all, and to the spirits of just men made perfect." Our Messiah did bring manna for He declared unto the Pharisees, "This is that bread which came down from heaven: not as your fathers did eat manna, and are dead: he that eateth of this bread shall live for ever" (John 6:58).

Not one "jot or tittle" of the prophecies concerning the Messiah's first advent was left unfulfilled or postponed. The early disciples found it difficult to comprehend the spiritual fulfillment of the Jewish traditional dream. And to our great sorrow, disciples of the twentieth century still cry for a materialistic, political, Jewish regime to satisfy their fleshly minds. Christ has no desire to reign on political thrones, for His "kingdom is not of this world" (John 18:36). Rather, He pleads for a throne in the souls of human beings. Our Messiah occupies the throne of His father, David, which is the sovereign rule over spiritual Israel, the church, and in far greater glory than David's reign over literal Israel.

Man's ego and carnal craving still blind his spiritual eyes, and he continues to dream of earthly glories. The roots of the Jewish traditions which Jesus condemned have been fertilized with contemporary fantasy resulting in the growth of a millennial teaching which deceives many Christians. After revising the old Jewish dreams, numerous speculations have been added. Millennial teachers prophesy the restoration of Jerusalem with a temple for the Messiah. This erroneous doctrine stems from a misinterpretation of the twentieth chapter of Revelation.

The Binding of Satan

(See Picture Chart following page 32: Strip 5)

The Revelation depicts seven parallel themes, portraying various phases of the church established at Christ's first advent and climaxing at His second coming; chapter twenty presents the final theme. The nineteenth chapter concludes with the bride prepared for the Bridegroom, and the final judgment and doom of the wicked. John begins a new theme in chapter twenty commencing again with the first century and tracing the prophecies of the church to the final consummation.

John the Revelator visualizes an angel from heaven taking a great chain in his hand and binding Satan, the old serpent, the dragon, the Devil. The angel casts him into a bottomless pit,

shuts him up and sets a seal upon him for a thousand years so
that he cannot deceive the nations. Premillennialists claim that
this means Christ, in physical form, is casting down Satan incarnate in flesh, a half man, half beast creature. Now I refuse to
believe that an incarnate Devil has more vitality than incarnate
God. Jesus died within a few hours on the cross; but false teachers claim that this Devil is so invulnerable that even though he be
submerged in a bottomless pit for one thousand years he will not
die!

Centuries had passed, civilizations had come and gone.
Satan had deceived multitudes and the Messiah had not come.
Then in God's time Jesus came to free the people and release
souls bound in sin. Christ must bind Satan then deliver people
from Satan's power. The greatest battle ever fought was between
Jesus on the cross and Satan with all the powers of earth and
hell. If our Lord had not won the battle the whole world would
be lost forever. When Christ arose from the dead the victory was
won.

The entire book of Revelation is understood as symbolic
language. Our key of interpretation has served well and is proved
also by historical evidence. Now at the end of the great apocalypse it would be foolish to try to make a literal application of
figurative language.

This is not the first time a great red dragon, called the Devil
and Satan, appears in the Revelation. We saw this ugly creature
in chapter twelve with a fuller description. He comes to view
with seven heads, ten horns, and a tail that casts the stars of
heaven to the earth. It is quite absurd to literalize such a creature.
He is pictured as devouring the newly born nation of Christians
of the first century, as soon as they are born. This reveals the
heathen powers of Pagan Rome which Satan controlled and used
to fight against Christianity in its infancy.* The seven heads and

---

*Ezek. 29:3; Jer. 51:34—It is significant that enemies of God's people in
the Old Testament (Pharaoh and Nebuchadnezzar were also referred to as
dragons.

horns are identified as seven consecutive governing powers over Rome, and the ten horns are symbols of Rome in its decemregal form. This persecuting empire is called the Devil which means "accuser," and Satan which means "Adversary," because it was the very power of the king of hell which governed its cruel actions. When John said to the church at Smyrna, "Fear none of those things which thou shalt suffer: behold the devil shall cast some of you into prison, that ye may be tried" (Rev. 2:10a), he did not refer to Beelzebub in human form literally persecuting persons. It was the political power of Rome which cast the Christians into prison. It was named the Devil and Satan because it enacted his power so expertly.

Chapter twelve depicts the struggle between paganism and Christianity as a war where Michael, the angel, struggles with the dragon. Michael was the guardian angel to protect the Jewish people. They believed that the unseen angel's presence accompanied Israel in time of war. John is simply saying that as Michael was the tutelar angel of Israel, Christ is the unseen power of protection for the church in conflict against heathen paganism. What a comfort for early martyrs to know that Christ was with them in persecution and death. "Angel" being interpreted means "messenger." God's messengers, His ministers, are endowed with the Spirit of God and given power to cast down the works of Satan. Chronologically this scene takes place on this side of Calvary, after the blood was shed. The church is seen overcoming the dragon power of Satan by the "blood of the Lamb and by the word of their testimony; and they loved not their lives unto the death" (Rev. 12:11). The Christ who had promised never to leave His disciples kept His word. The Holy Spirit, the Comforter, that Jesus promised to send, came as He had said. Thus the Spirit of God worked through the church while the spirit of Satan controlled the powers of Pagan Rome.

The key in the angel's hand is a symbol of authority. When Christ gave the disciples the keys of the kingdom, they were not only commissioned to "open" the kingdom but also to "bind" the powers of sin. The only power in the world that is great enough to bind Satan is the power of God, the gospel of truth, proclaimed in the kingdom of God. The authority of God was placed upon the church to overthrow the evil forces of paganism.

The Word of God is the chain provided for the church to bind Satan. This chain of truth is composed of many links; the strength of the gospel chain is dependent upon each link being securely interlocked in unity. The Christian doctrines of the church are as mighty links. Repentance is interlocked with regeneration, baptism, and sanctification. The length of the chain increases with links of the ordinances of communion and foot washing, divine healing, tithing, and the unity of God's people. To these God added powerful links of faith including the doctrine of immortality, Christ's second coming, the last judgment, and the firm belief in heaven and hell. It is easy to recognize that John is saying that the church conquered Satan by the power of God's two witnesses. The angel is the **Spirit,** the chain is the **Word;** and it was accomplished by the authority of heaven as the key. Pagan teachings of heathenism became bound and powerless when the early apostles proclaimed truth accompanied by the Holy Spirit. The heathen gods, demi-gods, atheism, superstitions, and pagan teachings crumbled and fell under the grip and power of truth. The darkness was banished and the true light appeared. Heathen temples were forsaken, and in one generation the church prevailed to cast down Satan that he should no longer deceive the world with doctrines of hell. That is why John exclaimed, "And I heard a loud voice saying in heaven, Now is come salvation, and strength, and the kingdom of our God, and the power of his Christ: for the accuser of our brethren is cast down, which accused them before our God day and night" (Rev. 12:10).

Satan is a defeated foe. In the wilderness of temptation Jesus overcame the Devil's power. Jesus said ,". . . if I with the finger of God cast out devils, no doubt the kingdom of God is come upon you" (Luke 11:20). At Calvary Satan was cast down.

"Now is the judgment of this world: now shall the prince of this world be cast out. And I, if I be lifted up from the earth, will draw all men unto me" (John 12:31, 32). On the resurrection morning Jesus gave proof that He has all power in life and death.

God gave the early church great victory. The Christians, having received the Holy Spirit, were given power over Satan and turned the world upside down. God never fails to give great victory to those who obey Him. When you are in Christ there are not enough devils to make you sin. Satan can't make you lie, steal, hate, commit adultery, or rob you of your salvation . . . ". . . we shall reign on the earth" (Revelation 5:10b).

The god of the state lost its supremacy. The God of heaven and earth was acknowledged above Caesars. Heathen idols of Diana, the virgin goddess of the moon; Venus, the goddess of love; Mars, the war god; Bacchus, the god of wine; Zeus, the supreme deity among the Greeks; and innumerable others were abandoned. The world became as nominally Christian as it had been pagan. Thus, cast down in political and religious authority, the devil of paganism is described as being in a bottomless pit. A bottomless pit indicates an abyss of darkness with no end to it. Seven times it appears in the Revelation and always refers to habitation of beastly enemies of the church. The final doom of all evil is described as being cast into this bottomless pit which is eternal—having no end. This dragon bequeaths his power, seat, and great authority over to the beast of Catholicism; but, heathen powers, as such, no longer deceive the world. The fact that the dragon gave his power, seat, and authority over to the beast of Catholicism is evidence that the dragon is not Beelzebub in person—he has never abdicated as yet!

The Reign of the Martyrs

Paul frequently writes in his Epistles about reigning in this life with Christ. To the Romans he wrote, "For if by one man's offense death reigned by one; much more they which receive abundance of grace and of the gift of righteousness shall reign in life by one, Jesus Christ" (Rom. 5:17). He further explains that "sin shall not have dominion over you" (Rom. 6:14a). Thus the Christian reigns over sin, self, and Satan in this present world; even while Satan is going to and fro, "seeking whom he may devour" (1 Pet. 5:8). We reign over Satan "because greater is he that is in you, than he that is in the world" (1 John 4:4b). Saints throughout the centuries received the power of the Holy Spirit which enabled them to reign over temptation and sin, and to even face death triumphantly.

John sees heaven's curtain pulled back, and gets a glimpse into the paradise of God. Here he visualizes the souls of multitudes who suffered death as martyrs, continuing their reign with Christ; "willing rather to be absent from the body, and to be present with the Lord" (2 Cor. 5:8b). These are the souls John saw under the altar of God when the fifth seal was opened (Rev. 6:9-11). John again describes them as the souls "beheaded for the witness of Jesus, and for the word of God, and which had not worshipped the beast, neither his image, neither had received his mark upon their foreheads, or in their hands; and they lived and reigned with Christ a thousand years" (Rev. 20:4). God was not asleep when millions were tortured, persecuted, and slain by pagan, papal, or Protestant powers. Those beheaded by earthly rulers were honored and seated with Christ in glory. Not a word is here mentioned of Christ reigning on the earth. While the earthly reign of the church was eclipsed and millions of Christians were slain, it is written, "Blessed are the dead which die in the Lord from henceforth: Yea, saith the Spirit, that they may rest from their labors; and their works do follow them" (Rev. 14:13b). This is the blessed estate of the righteous, who, like Stephen, saw heaven open, and the Son of God standing to receive them into paradise. Does not the Bible say, "If we suffer, we shall also reign with him" (2 Tim. 2:12a)? This was the faith of the martyrs; they firmly believed the promise of Christ saying, "To him that overcometh will I grant to sit with me in my throne, even as I also overcame, and am set down with my Father in his throne" (Rev. 3:21).

The church was born on a battlefield with many conflicts. The Lord is faithful. "The gates of hell shall not prevail against it." There have been martyrs for the Christian faith in every decade. It is so disturbing to learn of an increase in the number of Christians who are martyrs in our world today. An International Day of Prayer for the Persecuted Church was observed November 16th, 1997. In 1996, an estimated 160,000 Christians around the world were martyred. In fact, more Christians have been martyred in the 20th century than in the past 19 centuries combined. On November 16, 1997 more than 50,000 churches, synagogues, and other groups in the U.S., as well as people from 115 nations participated.

Richard Wurmbrand, a Romanian pastor empowered by God to serve the persecuted church worldwide, survived fourteen years of torture for Christ in Communist prisons. Pastor Wurmbrand and his wife Sabina continue to visit Christians in chains and challenge free Christians to action through The Voice of the Martyrs ministry they helped to found. Let me share Pastor Wurmbrand's letter to the Western church in the publication, *"The Voice of the Martyrs"* (November 1997, p. 2) in which he asks, "Why should I weep?"

The Voice of the Martyrs

Dear brothers and sisters,

"And whoever lives and believes in Me shall never die" (John 11:26).

Let me tell you about a girl my wife, Sabina, met while she was in prison.

Sabina was in a prison cell with some twenty or thirty ladies. Among them was a young girl of perhaps twenty who had been sentenced to death for her faith.

Her day had come to be executed. The executions always took place at midnight. It was her last evening, and the guards had brought in some food. All of the women in the cell were hungry but no one cared to eat, as they all pitied this beautiful, young girl.

Then her face began to shine.

She lifted the dishes of food and said, "I have a fiancé. I love him wholeheartedly and he loves me. He hoped that one day I would be in his embraces. But tonight I will be shot and, after a few hours, my body will become clay just like the clay out of which this dish has been made. Who knows what has gone into it? Perhaps what has been the dreaming eye of a lover?

"After a few more years my body will have decomposed, but my spirit will not die. I have had many physical bodies, such as that of an embryo, an infant, a young girl, and now a woman. But I am an eternal spirit, and that cannot be killed. Jesus said, 'Whoever lives and believes in Me shall never die' and I believe these words of Jesus. I believe them more than the rifles, which will be stretched out. I believe these words of Jesus more than the bullets, which will enter my heart. I believe these words of Jesus more than the open grave, which awaits me.

"For me this grave is the doorway to a heavenly city. Who can tell the beauty of that city? There, sadness is not known. No one ever weeps or sighs. There is only joy and song. Everyone is dressed in the white of purity. We can see God face to face. There are such joys that human language cannot express."

A few minutes before midnight, the prison guards came to take her. As she walked toward her "death," she began reciting the Christian creed. We have seen Christians walking to their execution with songs on their lips. They were going to their Beloved One. "Why should I weep? Why should I be sad?"

It is a joy for them to sacrifice themselves for Christ, knowing that Christ has sacrificed Himself for them. Love has been His promise. How terrible to marry when one loves and the other does not. How terrible when Christ loves us and we do not love Him. He loves us with a flame of ardent love; so must our love be for Him.

The ladies who had remained behind in the prison were in tears. They heard a few shots. The poor Communists believed that they had killed her. They did not know that they had sent her into the embraces of her Heavenly Bridegroom.

We have eternal life through Christ. All those who put their trust in God, the great Father, can be happy and joyous because our life will be eternal. That is the message that I bring you out of prisons in captive nations.

I usually disappoint my readers. Everyone has heard that I have been in jail for many years and when I preach they expect to hear a melancholy preacher with a very sad face, telling them how much he has suffered. Go and look for such faces somewhere else. We have the joy and peace of God. Hands that have worn chains are hands that can bless, and I bring you the blessings of your brethren in captive nations.

Remember them in your prayers. Love them with all your heart. Open your hearts to receive the beauty of their example. Those who are Christians begin a new Christian life. It should not be lukewarm; it should not be a shadow of the reality of Christ. True Christianity is to be a flame of fire. As He has left heaven for us and died on Golgotha, so we belong to Him in love and in faith. He should be our song.

I know that you have sorrow and pain but, as often as the sorrow comes, you can sing.

As Jesus walked toward the garden of Gethsemane, He knew that Judas would arrive and betray Him. He knew that the apostles would desert Him. He knew that He would be whipped until He bled. He knew that they would drive nails into His hands and feet. He knew that He would hang in terrible suffering on a cross. He knew that He would see His mother weeping at the foot of the cross. But despite all this, He and the apostles sang a hymn and departed (Matt. 26:30).

After our sorrows and pains, there will also be a resurrection. Love God with all your heart. Believe in the forgiveness of sin that Christ gives. Start a life of love in the power of the Holy Spirit. How beautiful it will be when we will be with Christ for eternity!

I wish I were a painter, as I would have liked to paint all the beautiful faces of Christians in prison. Their faces radiated with joy, which was quite an achievement—only God could make a face shine there because they had not washed. I did not wash for three years, but the love of God shone from behind a crust of dirt.

They had a triumphant smile because they had the privilege of suffering for the Lord. I call upon you, dear brothers and sisters, if you wish to know the joy of Christ, take your crosses upon yourself. Jesus said, "If anyone desires to come after Me, let him deny himself, and take up his cross and follow Me" (Matt. 16:24). Discover the joy of following Jesus—wherever He leads.

Sincerely In Christ,
Richard Wurmbrand[1]

The Mysterious Thousand

"O For a *Thousand* Tongues To Sing. . . ." Charles Wesley expresses through the hymn that bears this title, a sincere desire to offer perfect praise. How vibrantly we extol the phrase, "If I had *ten thousand* lives with which to praise Him. . . ," endeavoring to exclaim boundless exaltation. This context is used in the song of the Hebrews offering praise with the words relating to God speaking, "For every beast of the forest is mine, and the cattle on a *thousand* hills. . . . For the world is mine, and the fulness thereof" (Psalm 50:10-12).

The term "thousand" is not used in a literal sense but in figurative speech to indicate vastness. We recall the psalmist conveying the truth of God's protection when he writes, "A *thousand* shall fall at thy side, and *ten thousand* at thy right hand; but it shall not come nigh thee" (Psalm 91:7). This expresses complete protection.

To give the Israelites a concept of God's covenant to multiply Abraham's seed, this description is used: "And I will make

---

[1]Wurmbrand, Richard, "Why Should I Weep? Why Should I Be Sad?" *The Voice of the Martyrs,* November 1997, p.2 (used by permission).

thy seed as the dust of the earth: so that if any man can number the dust of the earth, then shall thy seed also be numbered" (Genesis 13:16). Isaiah prophesied, ". . . thy people Israel be as the sands of the sea" (Isaiah 10:22). And in Deuteronomy 1:10-11, it is written, "The Lord your God hath multiplied you, and behold, ye are this day as the stars of heaven for multitude. (The Lord God of your fathers make you a *thousand times* so many more as ye are, and bless you as He hath promised you!") The dust, sands, and stars are innumerable and "a *thousand* times more" meant to be multiplied a thousand-fold.

John, the Revelator, employs this description for the new covenant God made with the new Israel, the church. Twelve is the number for the church. As there were twelve tribes in literal Israel, John refers to the church in the same figure of speech to include all God's chosen people. The square of twelve is one hundred forty-four and the term *"thousand"* is used to denote the number of the redeemed is multiplied a *thousand*-fold. After John lists all twelve tribes using *"thousand"* for each tribe making 144,000 in all, he then exclaims, "After this I beheld, and lo, a great multitude, which no man could number, of all nations, and kindreds, and people, and tongues stood before the throne, and before the Lamb . . ." (Revelation 7:9). The *thousand* indicates innumerable. "Twelve *thousand* is used numbers of times in the scriptures. Ten stands for a rounded total. Thus we have ten commandments and the ten plagues. *Thousand* is the cube of ten and to multiply a thousand-fold indicates vast completeness. Example: "Behold, the Lord cometh with ten *thousand* of his saints, to execute judgment . . ." (Jude 14, 15). When John describes the Holy City, he speaks of twelve *thousand* furlongs (Revelation 21:14). Literally it would indicate a cube city of 1400 miles, approximately sufficient room for about 144,000 inhabitants. It is understood John employs the language of ancient prophets in the term *"thousand."* Who could measure the actual size of heaven? *Thousand* implies immeasurable.

The use of the term *"thousand"* is quite well accepted with spiritual application for numbering God's possessions, God's people, and measuring the place He is preparing for His children. However, when it comes to a measure for God's time table there is a reluctance. "Time" is frequently expressed without exact clock or calendar calculations. When we refer to the "hour of temptation" (Revelation 3:10) or Jesus says, "the hour is come; glorify thy Son . . ." (John 17:1), it is not giving reference to sixty minutes. To speak of a "day" often is not referring to twenty-four hours. The "day of creation" means from the beginning of creation until all things were created. The "old testament day" ended with the coming of Jesus. It is interesting to note the prayer of Moses (Psalm 90:4), "For a *thousand* years in thy sight are but as yesterday when it is past, and as a watch in the night." Peter picks up the phrase saying "one day with the Lord is as a *thousand* years, and a *thousand* years is as one day" (II Peter 3:8). We often express "gospel day," "day of salvation," or "day of grace." Indeed, it is common to speak of one's lifetime as "my day" or "your day."

The prophets of the Revelation are on God's timetable from the first to the second coming of Christ. This period is known as the "day of Grace." It is the "Messianic Day," the Messiah has come! The "Gospel Day" began with Christ's first advent and will conclude at His Second Coming. John refers to this period of the Kingdom of God on earth as a *thousand* years, the "Gospel Day." John's figurative context of *"thousand"* in reference to the number of the redeemed (Revelation 7) and to the measurements of the Holy City, (Revelation 21) is also expressed in chapter twenty depicting the spiritual reign of the church during this day of grace.

Another word for "thousand" is the millennium. Our religious world is altogether too materialistic in the concept of the kingdom. Christ came to establish a reign in the hearts of men, not a political empire. Messianic prophecies have been fulfilled at our Lord's first advent. The new creation is His church. Lions and lambs lie down together as sinful natures are redeemed by His blood. Christ is greater than Moses, giving the true Bread from heaven rather than manna. Whosoever will call upon the Name of the Lord can be saved. Christ, our Messiah, brought the greatest peace. The Holy Spirit has been poured out upon God's people. The New Testament is sealed with Christ's blood at Calvary, and the gospel is preached to all the world.

At the first coming of our King He bound and cast Satan down from his reign of deception. Jesus speaks of binding the strong man, entering his house, and taking his spoils (Matthew 12:25-29). Our Lord entered the world which had been deceived by Satan for centuries, dethroned Satan, and released souls from the prison of sin. He said, "If I cast out devils by the Spirit of God, then the kingdom of God is come unto you" (Matthew 12:28). John records that nearing the end of our Lord's earthly ministry, He utters, "Now is the judgment of this world: now shall the prince of this world be cast out. And I, if I be lifted up from the earth will draw all men unto me" (John 12:31-32). Since Calvary all millennial blessings have been available to the Christian.

John places a sharp focus on the beginning and ending of the gospel day. He contrasts the first century church with the last century believers in repeated parallel themes. The prophecies depict a long apostasy between the beginning and ending, but a restored church at the end of the gospel day. The revelator recaps this theme in Revelation 20. He portrays Christ's first coming to destroy Satan's power, bind Satan's deception by the power of the Holy Spirit, and proclaim the gospel to all nations. He envisions the Christians who reign over sin, self, and Satan, as rulers on thrones with Christ. These souls who reign have died to sin, are alive to Christ, and have no marks or identification with Satan, the beast. Even during periods of persecution in the dark ages physical death could not rob souls of their of righteousness with our Lord.

The spotlight then focuses on the end of the *thousand* years. Just as we express "as the church was in the morning so shall it be in the evening," John prophesies that just as the church was confronted with Satan, the deceiver, as a political persecuting power against the church in the morning, he would be released at the close of the gospel day as an enemy to deceive the nations, and persecute the church in the evening of time.

It is observed that Satan was loosed—he did not break the chain that bound him. Truth is the chain that binds deception and error and truth cannot be broken. We may best understand this by a comparison of the judgment of God upon the antediluvian world. The gross wickedness of Noah's day is an example of signs of Christ's second coming, "As the days of Noah were, so shall also the coming of the Son of man be" (Matthew 24:37). Just before the flood God expressed "my spirit shall not always strive with man" (Genesis 6:3). God left man to his own destruction because he refused to repent. In like manner when the gospel is preached to the whole world and men continue to refuse His Holy Spirit, then God permits man's choice for deception. At the birth of Jesus it is estimated that less than one tenth of one percent of world population knew about one true God. All others were deceived. Christ came, the gospel is preached in all the world (There is no nation that is totally pagan.), but again the world has rejected God. World conditions are rapidly becoming like those in Noah's day.

The phrase "and when the *thousand* years are expired Satan shall be loosed" (Revelation 20:7), commands our attention. It is saying at the end of the Gospel day Satan shall be loosed. Since the term *"thousand"* indicates a vast indefinite period of time, the prophecy does not state that suddenly the world is deceived again. Satan's release is a gradual deception as man little by little rejects truth and light choosing darkness and evil. John explains this transpires at the ending of the day of grace. We are now living in the end of the *"thousand* years." Satan is now released to deceive the nations. It must be observed that with the rebirth of atheism, the revival of paganism, and the onslaught of communist aggregation, that Satan is released to deceive the nations.

The mysterious *thousand* is scripturally defined as the vast, indefinite, innumerable, immeasurable, inclusive, non-exact expression depicting God's possessions, people, heavenly abode, and spiritual reign.[2]

The First Resurrection

It is readily understood that there are two kinds of birth—the physical and the spiritual. There are also two kinds of life and two kinds of death. It is then of necessity that there must be two kinds of resurrection. In the parable Jesus gave of the prodigal son, the father exclaims when his son returns, ". . . my son was dead, and is alive again" (Luke 15:24a). This does not refer to physical death. Jesus also taught saying, "He that heareth my word, and believeth on him that sent me, hath everlasting life, and shall not come into condemnation; but is passed from death unto life" (John 5:24).

To pass from death unto life is a resurrection, but Jesus was not speaking here of physical death and resurrection. Rather He referred to the spiritual state of death, separation from God, and the resurrection of a sinner being made alive by believing in His words. Paul also refers to spiritual life and death when he writes, "And you hath he quickened, who were dead in trespasses and sins" (Eph. 2:1). Again, it is written, "Awake thou that sleepest, and arise from the dead, and Christ shall give thee light" (Eph. 5:14b).

The first resurrection is the deliverance of the soul from the death of sin to a new life in Jesus Christ. John said, "Blessed and holy is he that hath part in the first resurrection: on such the second death hath no power" (Rev. 20:6a). The only resurrection that can make one holy (without sin) is the new birth, salvation from the dead works of iniquity. John also wrote, "And death and hell were cast into the lake of fire. This is the second death" (Rev. 20:14a). The only resurrection that can save one from the

[2]Lillie McCutcheon, *Vital Christianity*, May 27, 1979.

second death of being cast into hell is the resurrection from sin unto righteousness.

The early church proclaimed this glorious truth of the first resurrection. Multitudes were delivered from the graves of spiritual death and received the abundant life Jesus came to give to all who received Him. It is evident, however, that during the apostasy, the truth of a spiritual resurrection was very obscure, while a religion of dead works became very prominent. The prophecy proclaims that after the long period of spiritual death in the world there would again come another reign upon the earth. This was fulfilled with the reformation being ushered in, restoring again the proclamation of the spiritual resurrection. The true church in the evening time declares the same spiritual resurrection from dead works to new life in Christ, as was proclaimed in the morning church.

The Dragon Released

There is a shout of triumph in the soul of every saint who understands the prophecies of God's church being restored in the evening of time. When the Dark Ages of Roman Catholicism rolled away and the dark and cloudy day of Protestantism faded, God's children rejoiced in the evening light. Zechariah's words, "but it shall come to pass, that at evening time it shall be light" (Zech. 14:7b), are being fulfilled in our day.

It is exciting to see the same Lamb of God which was sacrificed in the morning of the gospel day appearing again near the ending of the day on Mount Zion and being worshipped by a mighty host of saints. The pure woman seen in the morning time, hidden in the Dark Ages, comes to prominent view as a bride in the evening. The same two witnesses, the Spirit and the Word, are prophesied as being equally as active in the world at the closing of the gospel day as they were in the beginning.

However, it must also be observed that the same dragon of heathenism which persecuted the Christians in the early church is also released and appears as an enemy of the church in the evening time. The prophecies tell, "And when the thousand years are expired, Satan shall be loosed out of his prison, and shall go out to deceive the nations which are in the four quarters of the earth" (Rev. 20:7-8a).

The reason Satan was bound was to take away his power to deceive the world. The evil deception was taken away when Jesus proclaimed the truth and established His kingdom. He said, "This gospel of the kingdom will be preached in the whole world as a testimony to all nations, and then the end will come" (Matthew 24:14). The power to bind Satan was the Holy Spirit and the Word of God. This power was given to the church. Satan does not get loose on his own strength. When the church fails to let the Spirit work through them and proclaim the truth of the Word, to that measure Satan gets free.

We have learned that Satan is the evil enemy. He tried to destroy the church as soon as it was born. He is a liar. The Devil worked through the powers of the Jews and Romans to kill Christians. Pagan religions were commanded while saints were persecuted. In our lifetime Communism is very much like Pagan Rome. Thank God much of the evil of Communism has been conquered, but it is far from being dead.

How utterly futile to believe that such diabolical powers of Satan could be conquered with weapons of carnal warfare. Winston Churchill has said, "Communism is a riddle wrapped up in an enigma." Christians must observe that this is a spiritual struggle of ideologies. The enemy is using political force to seize the world, but victory for the free world can only be won by the spiritual power of our God. The Holy Spirit with the great chain of the Word is the only power sufficient to bind the pagan dragon.

The book of Genesis relates that from the beginning Satan has been likened unto a serpent beguiling the souls of men and women. All through the Bible he is seen deceiving and devouring the multitudes; indeed, the only souls to escape his evil power are those who have been redeemed. This treacherous devil of iniquity has transformed himself to appear in many different characters using religious and political powers as tools in his hands. The Revelation brings to view the final acts of war that Satan imposes against the church. The church of the first century had divine power to cast down and defeat this pagan, idolatrous force of Satan. According to the prophecies this demon power is now released again.

Already in our day the anti-god forces have claimed the lives of millions of Christians;[3] at this writing, it is estimated that at least seventeen million Christians are in concentration camps behind the iron or bamboo curtains. Is this the end? No—many more must join the ranks of Christian martyrs.

The *Pulpit Digest* relates the following:

> In our American church we find few Christians who have ever been called upon to suffer for Christ. Our church has yet to be tried in the fire seven times. We have not known what it is to experience discomfort for our faith to say nothing of real suffering. But there are names in our time which could make up a modern "Book of Martyrs." A returning missionary tells us of a Presbyterian elder of Korea who could walk in the company of Stephen. His witness was made as the tide of war was rushing back and forth over the 32nd parallel in Korea.
>
> When the Communist forces moved into South Korea, they brought with them iron weapons and the cruel wills of persecution. They seized this elder, bound his wrists with thongs and lined him up against the wall to shoot him because he was a Christian. He asked the officers in charge of the firing squad if he might have his wrists unbound so that he could die a free man. The officer nodded; there was a flash of steel in the sunlight as a bayonet cut not only the thongs, but also severed his hands from his arms at the same time. Turning about and facing the firing squad, he lifted his mangled arms from which his blood was spurting and gave his enemies this benediction: "Unto God's gracious mercy and protection we commit you. And the blessing of God Almighty, the Father, the Son and the Holy Spirit be upon you and remain with you

---

[3]*Native Missionary Publication* places the figure at 20-30 million.

forever." Then the guns of the firing squad spoke and he fell dead.[4]

Only God knows how many more must seal their faith with their own blood. There is a ray of light in the prophecies. It is written, "that he [the dragon] must be loosed a **little** season" (Rev. 20:3b). There is no prediction in the prophecies for another long period of dark ages. Rather it says that when the enemies of the church encamped about the beloved city (the church) that "fire came down from God out of heaven, and devoured them" (Rev. 20:9). Some have supposed this fire to represent revival flames of truth burning and consuming error, infidelity and division, and producing a great body of Christians purged from traditionalism and sectarianism. Others maintain that this is the fire of judgment and wrath of God. Either and probably both may be true. The church is restored completely and the bride is made ready before the Lord's coming. It is also true that at the Master's return final doom and judgment is poured out upon Satan— that old serpent. The dragon is last seen when he is eternally cast into the bottomless pit of hell. "And the devil that deceived them was cast into the lake of fire and brimstone, . . . and shall be tormented day and night for ever and ever" (Rev. 20:10). The Christ will reign forever and ever and all his saints shall arise to reign with Him for millenniums that have no end!

---

[4]*Pulpit Digest,* November, 1955, p. 61.

CHAPTER VII

THE BATTLE OF ARMAGEDDON

John the Revelator charts the prophecies of the church from the first century until the Lord's appearing. The four Gospels reveal the lifetime of the physical body of Christ from birth to heaven's portals. In like manner the Revelation portrays the earthly life-span of the spiritual body of Christ, the church, from birth to eternity. Most of John's prophecies have reached their fulfillment. The position of the church in this century is nearing the close of the age. To even pinpoint our position of today, we find ourselves as participants in prophetic fulfillment. Today we stand at Armageddon!

Literally, Armageddon is the name of an ancient battlefield at the foot of Mount Megiddo in Palestine. Here the Jews fought numerous battles. On this site Saul took his life; here Deborah and Barak sang a song of victory; and it marks the place where Sisera and his great armies were defeated. The Plain of Armageddon is only twenty miles wide and about forty-five miles long. Indeed, the whole country of Palestine is very small— approximately 9,000 square miles, about one-fourth the size of the state of Indiana.

It is utterly preposterous to conceive of Christians fighting a literal battle in this small area when the battle of Armageddon is to be the greatest, largest, and final battle of the church.

Remembering that the Old Testament gave literal pictures which serve as shadows of spiritual fulfillment in the New Testament church, let us discover an Old Testament story which symbolizes today's Armageddon.

In the year 164 B.C., the Grecian Empire endeavored to force the entire known world to become Hellenistic. Judas Maccabee, the Hammer, was a leader of Jewish priests who defended the Jewish religion. At Armageddon this small number of Jewish priests fought Lysias, General of Antiochus Epiphanes and his mighty army.[1] It was a battle of horror and much bloodshed. Gog and Magog, referred to in Ezekiel, chapter 39, were enemies of the Jews who joined the forces of destruction against Jerusalem. But God was with His people, the Jews, and even though they were small in number they won the victory. The Grecian enemy was defeated and the Jewish kingdom was restored to a glory almost comparable to Solomon's splendor. This was known as the Asmonean dynasty. With the understanding of this literal battle as a type, it is not difficult to comprehend the spiritual antitype.

In the Revelation, chapters 15 and 16, John tells of seven vials of wrath being poured out upon the earth. Five of these plagues have already passed as judgments of God, and today we are encountering the sixth. In John's vision he beholds the vial of wrath being poured out upon the river, Euphrates. Literally this river flowed through the center of ancient Babylon. When Babylon, the mighty empire, was destroyed, the enemy gained entrance inside the city by diverting the course of the river and marching in on the riverbed. The vial John speaks of as being poured out on the Euphrates is indicative of God's wrath being poured out on spiritual Babylon preceding her final destruction.

John says, "And I saw three unclean spirits like frogs come out of the mouth of the dragon, and out of the mouth of the beasts, and out of the mouth of the false prophet. For they are the spirits of devils, working miracles, which go forth unto the kings of the earth and of the whole world, to gather them to the battle of that great day of God Almighty. Behold, I come as a thief. Blessed is he that watcheth, and keepeth his garments, lest he walk naked, and they see his shame. And he gathered them together into a place called in the Hebrew tongue Armageddon" (Rev. 16:13-16). It is evident that a spiritual battle is here in-

---

[1]Brown, C. E., *Reign of Christ*; Warner Press, Anderson, Indiana, p. 179.

dicated, since the foe is likened unto three unclean spirits—slippery, slimy and sly—like frogs. These evil spirits encounter the whole world; the arena encompasses the globe.

It is significant that the church was born on a battlefield; her warfare has filled the pages of history in every generation, and she is seen at the end of time entrenched in her most vicious battle—Armageddon! Three great wars have been fought—and won by true Christianity. The first was a struggle with the dragon of paganism; the second was with the beast of papalism; the third was an encounter with the evils of the false prophets. In the final conflict, the church is faced with all three as a trinity of evil. Satan has combined his forces in the final attempt to destroy the church.

The church is at war! War against all evil. God is gathering His Army preparing for the final conflict of the ages.

Christianity is the oldest religion in the world. Salvation is the "mystery angels desired to look into." It is written ". . . the Lamb that was slain from the creation of the world" (Revelation 13:8 NIV). Jesus purchased the church with His blood at Calvary. Satan thought he had won the war when Jesus was crucified. God, our Father, had other plans and Jesus arose from the grave conquering death.

Satan tried to drown the church with martyrs' blood. Nero tried to kill the church by killing Christians. The powers of Romanism fought the church with persecution and death for the long period of more than twelve hundred and sixty years. This was the longest war of history. In the year A.D. 612 Mohammedanism attacked the church with severe punishment when the Christians refused to accept the Koran. Many false prophets, cults and Satan worshippers have deceived multitudes. A sectarian spirit has divided God's people, but the church still lives.

The true church includes every born again Christian. God keeps the record of membership. Paul, the Apostle, gives the requirements for all Christian soldiers: "Put on the full armor of God so that you can take your stand against the devil's schemes.

For our struggle is not against flesh and blood, but against the rulers, against the authorities, against the spiritual forces of evil in the heavenly realms. Therefore put on the full armor of God, so that when the day of evil comes, you may be able to stand your ground, and after you have done everything, to stand. Stand firm then, with the belt of truth buckled around your waist, with the breastplate of righteousness in place, and with your feet fitted with with the readiness that comes from the gospel of peace. In addition to all of this, take up the shield of faith, with which you can extinguish all the flaming arrows of the evil one" (Ephesians 6:11-18 NIV).

I was delighted recently while reading an article about revival in Christianity. It was startling to learn how many religions were being revived. The shinto priests have persuaded many Japanese to return to the pagoda. Eighty percent of converts were not Japanese. The worldwide charismatic movement has tripled in the last decade to nearly 300 million, including millions of Catholics. Jews are expecting their Messiah in the year 2000. Mormons report their large gains in membership. The New Age movement is expanding. New approaches are made by the Arab world. Islam fundamentalists see revival. In Buddhism there is new life. Bahaism, a cult offshoot from Mohammedanism originating in Persia, is making rapid growth. It is reported the United States alone has 3000 different religious beliefs. This is just a few statistics about our Religious World.

John, the Revelator, describes his vision about Armageddon. To my knowledge the name "Armageddon" appears only this one time in the Bible (Rev. 16:13).

Three Evil Spirits

I. *Communism*

The first of the unclean spirits is breathed out of the mouth of the "dragon." This presents another description of the dragon being "loosed" for a little season. The dragon of paganism breathed out of its foaming nostrils the deadly spirit of communism. More satanic than Pagan Rome, this treacherous force of iniquity is determined to exterminate Christianity.

We thank the Lord for the great change in Russia. The door has opened to let Christianity in. The Berlin Wall is broken. However, Communism is still alive. The deadly red dragon of atheism continues in North Korea, China, Cuba, Vietnam and other places of persecution. Don Hillis writes concerning his missionary work in China regarding Pastor Wang:

Even his congregation wouldn't recognize him from a little distance. His face is unshaven, his hair disheveled, and his clothes are shabby and smelly as if he hadn't had a good bath for some time. He is wandering aimlessly down one of Peiping's narrow, noisy alleys. His name: Wang Ming Tao—beloved pastor of the largest congregation in this capitol city of Communist China.

This man of God is muttering over and over to himself, "I am Judas, I am Judas!" There is something haunting about the dark, drawn lines on the old man's face. His dark restless eyes stare out of their deep sockets with fear and suspicion. His agonizing, monotone repetition of "I am Judas, I am Judas," tears at your heart, and sends chills up and down your spine.

Desiring to comfort him, you say, "But Wang Ming Tao, you are not Judas. Your mind is simply playing tricks on you as a result of many weeks of imprisonment, slander, torture, false accusations, and brainwashing. You and your fellow Christians have been brutally treated by the Communists." "Oh, but I am Judas. I am Judas. I have denied my Lord," is his reply.

Pastor Wang was recently released from his prison cell after signing a "confession" of crimes he never committed. In a couple of months he recovered his physical and mental faculties. He then returned to the Communist authorities and renounced his "confession," and declared his loyalty to Jesus Christ. As a result, Pastor Wang Ming Tao and his wife were back in a dark Communist prison.[2]

---

[2]Hillis, Don, *Thirty Pieces of Silver,* Orient Crusades, Los Angeles, Calif.

II. *Catholicism*

The second unclean spirit comes out of the mouth of the beast of papalism. After more than a thousand years of papal supremacy throughout the world, the true church conquered and the mighty Reformation of the sixteenth century released true Christians from papal bondage. What a victory was wrought by the Holy Spirit and Sacred Scripture. The prophecies tell that just before the end of time, this papal power will strike again against the true church in a final lunge for power. Anyone who is aware of conditions in Catholic-controlled countries couldn't be ignorant of the fact that Catholicism is an enemy of true Christian faith, and the real Christian church is her target.

I am confident God has a number of sincere Christians in Catholicism. They have done many good humanitarian deeds.

Politically, the Roman Catholic regime endeavors to train a Roman Catholic person for every political post in local, state, and federal offices. The Catholic church has always been known as a political power as well as a religious power. Catholics are taught not to believe in separation of church and state. They maintain that the pope should rule all civil powers. Indeed, they believe the pope is Lord of the earth.

Educationally, already some twenty-one states have Roman Catholic nuns and priests on the public school payroll. Incidentally, these have to pay not one penny of income taxes—the church gets it all; whereas all Protestant ministers and teachers have to pay income tax. Nineteen states already give free transportation to parochial school students. In Chicago, 70 percent of the teachers are Roman Catholic while in New Orleans the percentage is 90. Roman Catholics are instructed to defeat all public school bond issues in order to force public schools to close. They exercise a large control over school curriculum. Catholic efforts have been successful in "purging" school books of historical events which present truth of Roman Catholic evils of the Dark Ages. More than four million boys and girls are enrolled in Roman Catholic schools. However, they are not content to supervise their own schools and scheme to receive educational funds, but they usurp authority in public school circles, dominating them also. It is estimated that the Roman church spends more than one billion dollars annually on its United States educational system alone.

Numbers of Negro citizens have been swept away in Catholic belief due to the educational evangelism program by Catholics for the south. Negro children denied education in white schools have been welcomed into Catholic institutions, increasing Catholic membership in America at an alarming rate.

Economically, the Roman church is one of the richest and most efficiently organized institutions in the world. Her wealth is fabulous! She counts her income in the billions of dollars and values her properties in the tens of billions. American Catholics send more money to support the Vatican than Catholics anywhere else in the world. There are 1,661 Catholic hospitals in the United States. The Roman church owns breweries, wine distilleries, hotels, factories, business establishments, laundries, bakeries and untold others. This is a dangerous, un-American policy to permit a foreign country to possess so much of America's wealth and real estate. The Vatican Estate in Italy is confined to 110 acres but in America her property is unmeasured. Rome's coffers are filled with money for penitence assessments, masses for purgatory victims and fees for religious services rendered. She also becomes rich on slave labor of her nuns, monks, and priests. But a chief source of revenue is from her liquor and gambling agencies. Her expenditure in America is comparatively small. She refuses to pay taxes. At this writing, thousands of dollars are owed to the United States government for taxes on California Breweries alone. She is always on the beggar side demanding the public to support her.

Socially, Rome is determined to force her way of life upon every phase of American living. She is making rapid strides to control the press. Almost every secular magazine or newspaper carries pictures, news comments and numerous articles of

Catholic religion. She gets more free publicity than any religion in the world. It is also alarming to find that the Roman Catholic church exerts authority over the freedom of the press in many areas. Rome's church has invaded the fields of television and radio in a preposterous measure. Most of the film and television personalities are Roman Catholic and use this opportunity to press their pattern of life upon the listening audience. Many Christians were shocked when the Catholics exerted sufficient power to keep the Martin Luther film off television in some areas.

The moral laxity of Roman Catholics is quite notorious in America as well as in foreign countries. Where true Christianity has consistently taken her stand against gambling, liquor intoxication, and sexual immorality, the Roman Catholic church has often winked at these sins.

It is also astounding to realize the power Catholicism wields in labor unions and business circles. Some businesses have been boycotted by Roman Catholics because they refused to donate money for Catholic building programs, fund raising projects, etc.

Religiously, the Roman Catholic church binds her subjects to ancient superstitions and heathen idolatry. The doctrine of purgatory is Satan's scheme to pour money into Rome's treasury, but worse still, it leads souls to believe they can attain salvation only after they die. It holds the sword of fear over its subjects until they are held by its dreadful power. To teach America's multitudes that salvation is attained by the individual's works is to preach false religion.

It is at this point that the Roman Catholic church is even more treacherous than communism. The Communists openly express no belief in God; the Roman Catholics claim the power and approval of God upon all their evil works. Through all ages they have been guilty of atrocious crimes which they claim have been done in the name of the Almighty God.

III. *Confederacy*

The least recognized of the three unclean spirits is the one breathed out of the mouth of the false prophet. Satan is a master at counterfeits. Communism is his counterfeit for God; Catholicism is the counterfeit for the church; and confederacy is the devil's counterfeit for Christian unity. The true church should be aware that Satan always comes to confuse the multitudes as soon as any truth has been revealed. When the sixteenth-century Reformation revived the truth that man is justified by grace through faith—a personal encounter with God as a new birth—then Satan presented church membership, a formal ceremony replacing a spiritual experience. When the Wesleys' teaching of the Holy Spirit infilling was sweeping the nations, Satan immediately set Christians at confusion regarding the experience. The church recognized a great revival of divine healing but has been confronted now with numbers of ministers who endeavor to bring healing through psychiatry. It is true that psychiatry has its place in our world, but it is disturbing to find ministers who deal more with their parishioner's minds than they do with their hearts and souls. Observing Satan's attack upon every truth restored to the church in the evening of time, it is not strange that a counterfeit for Christian unity should appear immediately following the revival of genuine truth concerning the oneness of God's children. It is always true that the counterfeit nearest to the genuine article is the most deceptive and dangerous.

Is this confederacy of denominations the answer to our Lord's prayer "that they all may be one"? Is the nature of the combined Protestant body of the nature of Christ? The Protestant body has chosen to make human creeds. Is the church to be humanly governed? Almost any Protestant church of any size will readily admit that they include in their membership some who are sinners and others who make no claim of being saints at all. Is the body of Christ composed of sinners and leaders who deny holiness?

The mouth of the false prophet utters all kinds of errors, cults, Satan worship, and division in the church. There is a spirit of independence, rebellion, and self will. Even church people are influenced by errors of humanism.

Humanism in the whole world has made its mark. The exaltation of the human self and debasing God is a tragic sin. It denies the deity of God, the inspiration of the scriptures, and the divinity of Jesus Christ. It denies the existence of the soul, life after death, salvation and heaven, damnation and hell. Humanism believes there are no absolutes, no right and wrong, that moral values are self-determined. It believes in sexual freedom between consenting individuals, regardless of age, including pre-marital sex, homosexuality, lesbianism, and incest.

Humanism believes in right to abortion, euthanasia, and suicide. It believes in equal distribution of America's wealth to reduce poverty and bring about equality. America's schools are contaminated with this philosophy. The world seeks a civilization without God, Christianity without Christ.[3]

There needs to be an honest study made concerning Christ's attitudes toward religious sects existing during His earthly ministry. Jesus believed many things the Pharisees believed, but He was not a Pharisee. He never excluded the Sadducees from His ministry, but He never became a Sadducee. Although He was sometimes identified with the sect of the Essenes, He never became one of them. Simon, the Zealot, became a follower of Christ, but Jesus never became a Zealot. He challenged Herodians to follow the way of the cross, but Jesus never became a party member of the Herodians.

Confederacy is an effort of a horizontal direction on the human level. Christian unity comes only by the perpendicular pull by the magnet of the Holy Spirit on a divine level.

Now the passage in Revelation is easily understood which reads: ". . . Satan [paganism] shall be loosed out of his prison, and shall go out to deceive the nations which are in the four quarters of the earth, Gog [Catholicism] and Magog [Protes-

---

[3]*Humanist Manifestos I and II*, Prometheus Books, Buffalo, N.Y.

tantism], to gather them together to battle: the number of whom is as the sand of the sea. And they went up on the breadth of the earth, and compassed the camp of the saints about, and the beloved city [the church]" (Rev. 20:7-9a).

Remember that Jesus warned His disciples concerning the destruction of literal Jerusalem saying, "And when ye shall see Jerusalem compassed with armies, then know that the desolation thereof is nigh" (Luke 21:20). We, as Christians, also know that when the armies of Satan are compassed about the church as a trinity of evil, the end of the world is nigh.

The trinity of evil is not confined to only its three unclean spirits. The dragon of paganism is evident in many other ways. There has been a revival of pagan Shintoism. Heathenism has been stirred again in Africa. The Mohammedans have erected a mosque in Washington, D.C., and consider America their most promising mission field. According to the *Christian Herald,* Hawaii is the first state in the U.S. to be a Buddhist stronghold with a number of Shinto shrines and several non-Christian sects.

Trends toward atheism are evident in many American colleges and institutions of learning. America becomes fertile for pagan beliefs when she forgets God. It is most certain that our nation will either be governed by God or choose the rule of a dictator, domestic or foreign born.

It is noted that even though the trinity of evil is of the same evil spirit, and controlled by Satan, each unclean spirit retains its own identity. When the end is pictured, there is still a dragon, a beast, and a false prophet. "And the devil that deceived them was cast into the lake of fire and brimstone, where the beast and the false prophet are, and shall be tormented day and night for ever and ever" (Rev.20:10).

The Columbus, Ohio *Dispatch* Newspaper, Friday, March 27, 1998, front page headlines read: SCHOLARS PLAN AUDACIOUS NEW TESTAMENT REWRITE. Excerpts are as follows:

"The Jesus Seminar, a group of scholars searching for the historical Jesus, plans to publish a 'new' New Testament next year that is likely to exclude the virgin birth, the resurrection and the entire book of Revelation.

"The seminar includes Bible scholars from Protestant, Roman Catholic and secular backgrounds.

"Other scholars disagree with the Jesus Seminar. Some contend the New Testament should be taken literally as history. Others believe the seminar has gone too far in casting out many Biblical traditions.

"Seminar co-founder Robert W. Funk, who will speak at Capital University tonight, also said the Jesus Seminar will participate in a 2000 A.D. 'canon council' on questions about dogma, including the Trinity, Jesus' divinity and formulation of new ways to think about God."

"Among members of the organization, the council is likened to the fourth-century Council of Nicea which adopted the Nicene Creed and established other church traditions. Unlike the Council of Nicea, the gathering in New York will have no power to set the policies of any church.

"Funk is former president of the Society of Biblical Literature and is director of the Westar Institute in Santa Rosa, Calif., where the Jesus Seminar is based.

"He said in an interview that scientific developments mean a new language is needed for references to God.

" 'Whoever or whatever God is has not changed. The majority of the people I know still believe in God in some sense.'

"A traditional, layer-cake view of the theological world with heaven above and hell below the earth 'can no longer be supported by what we now know of the structure of the universe,' he said.

"Most of the seminar's conclusions have originated with other scholars' findings, some dating back centuries.

" 'There is nothing new in what we are doing,' he said. Scholars used to keep the research to themselves, because 'we have been afraid of the public outcry, afraid of losing our jobs. A group of us got together and decided it was time to come clean. Our big aim was to get back into the public domain with serious Biblical scholarship.'

"The Rev. William C. Dettling, associate professor of dogmatic theology at the Pontifical College Josephinum, is a critic of the group.

"Funk knows the seminar's views on resurrection will be controversial.

" 'It has always amazed me that people believe they are entitled to live beyond death. It seems to be the thing which makes people unusual in the animal kingdom. We have no idea what happens after death. (The scriptures) are expressions of human aspiration.'

"The Jesus Seminar consists of more than 70 scholars from respected academic institutions.

Jesus Seminar Views:

"Jesus' public career lasted one to three years and He was not well received in His hometown. He infringed social codes, consorted openly with social outcasts, did not observe kosher or regularly practice fasting, did not observe purity codes and was at odds with His family, some of whom thought Him mad.

"In His lifetime, He was considered a healer but by modern standards the healings probably were of psychosomatic ailments.

"Something Jesus said or did in the temple probably led to His arrest and execution, not His claims to be the Messiah. The scholars believe there was no trial and New Testament stories about the trial were taken from Psalm 2. He probably was flogged by the Romans. The Romans, not the Jews, were guilty of Jesus' death.

"The story of Peter's denial is fiction.

"There was no resurrection of Jesus' body. It went the way of all corpses. Some of His followers did see visions of Him, but not until long after His death.

"Jesus was a Jew, not the first Christian. The real founders of traditional Christianity are Peter and Paul. Jesus did not intend to found a new religion and did not claim to be the son of God."[4]

THE TERM **antichrist** is quite popular in the vocabulary of the current religious world. It excites sensationalism, breeds apprehension, and creates appetite for mystical prophetic forecast. The media, study groups, evangelistic campaigns, and tape ministry, provide massive communication channels to spread strange concepts of antichrist. Some define antichrist as the Devil incarnate, half man and half beast. Others conclude the term refers to a political figure who will make a covenant with the Jews. There are those who believe it is old Lucifer himself. Indeed each generation labels individuals as their personification of antichrist!

---

[4]The Columbus, Ohio, *Dispatch* (Newspaper), Friday, March 27, 1998.

The Antichrist in Scripture

Rather than speculate and add more confusion, it will be best to let the Bible itself identify antichrist. It may be surprising to learn that only one author of the scriptures gives any mention of antichrist and that very briefly. It is difficult to conceive how the imagination could create such a wide variety of myths from only four short texts of scripture. John, the beloved disciple, never gives reference to antichrist in the Revelation or the Gospel that bears his name. Only in John's first and second epistle is it considered, as follows:

"Little children, it is the last time: and ye have heard that antichrist shall come, even now are there many antichrists; whereby we know that it is the last time" (I John 2:18). "Who is a liar but he that denieth that Jesus is the Christ? He is antichrist, that denieth the Father and the Son" (I John 2:22).

"And every spirit that confesseth not that Jesus Christ is come in the flesh is not of God: and this is the spirit of antichrist, whereof ye have heard that it should come; and even now already is it in the world" (I John 4:3).

"For many deceivers are entered into the world, who confess not that Jesus Christ is come in the flesh. This is a deceiver and an antichrist" (2 John 7).

Many Antichrists

Let us note the following observations:

1. John explains when antichrist would come by saying it would be characteristic of the "last time." The Scriptures define the "last time" or "last days" as beginning with the first coming of Christ. "God who at sundry times and in divers manners spake in times past unto the fathers by the prophets, Hath in these last days spoken unto us by his Son, whom he hath appointed heir of all things . . ." (Heb. 1:1, 2).

Since anti means "against" we observe that as soon as Christ was revealed in human flesh there were those who opposed Him. John explains that there were already many antichrist in the first century.

2. Nowhere in the Scripture does **antichrist** appear with a capital A or ever refer to a single individual as "The Antichrist." It does give reference to the "spirit of antichrist and the pronoun **it** is used.

3. John gives three marks of identification. He describes antichrist as a liar, denier, and deceiver. One major purpose of John's epistles is to give warning to the believers to beware of false teachers and erroneous doctrines. He is especially concerned with the heresy that denied Christ's coming in the flesh. John identifies false teachers as antichrists who deny the divinity, the incarnation, the atonement, the resurrection, and the ascension of Jesus Christ.

The basic fundamental of Christianity is established on **who** Christ is. Jesus was greatly concerned with "whom do men say that I the Son of man am?" (Matt.16:13). More important is the truth of who Christ is than what He said or did. He was not crucified because He healed the sick or spoke in parables but because "He made himself the Son of God" (John 19:7).

According to John's identification of antichrist, it is an inclusive term applied to all persons or religious beliefs lying, denying, and deceiving concerning who Jesus Christ really is.

When you add crime, drug addiction, murder, divorce, illegitimate sex, drunkenness, abuse, and the entire catalog of sins you see the battle we fight is against sin and Satan. You remember John saw in his vision "Spirits of devils working miracles, which go forth to the kings of the earth, and of the whole world, to gather them to the battle, of that great day of God Almighty" (Rev. 16:14). You will note the battlefield is the whole earth. The kings of the earth are in contrast with the kings in our Lord's Army. "And has made us kings and priests unto God" (Rev. 1:6). The Lord's Army is cautioned to watch and keep their garments. The Christian's garments are the whole armor of God.

Chapter VIII

JESUS IS COMING AGAIN

"I will come again, and receive you unto myself; that where I am, there you may be also" (John 14:3b). This is the promise of / our Lord. The angels confirm his words and utter to the disciples, "This same Jesus, which is taken up from you into heaven, shall so come in like manner as ye have seen him go into heaven" (Acts 1:11b). Christ's promise is repeated by the apostles and embraced by multitudes of saints in every generation.

This glorious prophecy shines like a diamond of light from the pages of Holy Writ. Sacred books of other religions are void of the jewels of prophecy. This is not difficult to understand. If human authors attempted with finite minds to foretell future events, they would leave behind them strong evidence of their deception. Only Almighty God grasps the ages. He is the Alpha and Omega. Our God knows all mysteries. None can deny that the prophecies in the Word of God find fulfillment in the march of the ages, corroborating God's prophetic statements.

When Jesus told His disciples that it was necessary for Him to go away but that He would return again, immediately they inquired when He would return. The Lord, the great Prophet, foretold a number of events that would transpire before His second advent. He said, "For many shall come in my name, saying, I am Christ; and shall deceive many" (Matt. 24:5). Concerning these false Christs, Josephus says, "there were many who, pretending to Divine inspiration, deceived the people, leading out numbers of them to the desert, pretending that God would show them the signs of liberty, meaning redemption from the Roman power; and that an Egyptian false prophet led 30,000 men into the desert, who were almost cut off by Felix." It was just judgment for God to deliver up that people into the hands of false Christs who had rejected the true One. The coming of false christs was to be one of the signs preceding the destruction of Jerusalem. However, throughout all the centuries, false leaders have repeatedly appeared claiming to be the Messiah.

Other prophecies that Jesus gave to warn the disciples of Jerusalem's destruction were of wars, famines, strange signs in the sky, persecution and apostasy. All these prophecies came to exact fulfillment, and then Jerusalem fell. The apostasy that our Lord depicted did not end with Jerusalem's destruction. The Lord said, "And because iniquity shall abound, the love of many shall wax cold. But he that shall endure unto the end, the same shall be saved" (Matt. 24:12-13). The apostles were deeply concerned regarding the rapid pace of the apostasy even before the end of the first century. Paul expressed his burdened soul when bidding farewell to the Ephesian elders saying, "For I know this, that after my departing shall grievous wolves enter in among you, not sparing the flock. Also of your own selves shall men arise, speaking perverse things, to draw away disciples after them" (Acts 20:29-30).

To the Thessalonians who anticipated the Lord's return in their lifetime Paul wrote: "Let no man deceive you by any means: for that day [Christ's coming] shall not come, except there come a falling away first, and that man of sin be revealed, the son of perdition; who opposeth and exalteth himself above all that is called God, or that is worshipped; so that he as God sitteth in the temple of God, shewing himself that he is God" (2 Thess. 2:3-4). Here is a prophecy that the anti-Christ and the apostasy would both precede the Lord's return. This "man of sin" could not refer to Caesar as some say. Caesar was already on the stage of history and Paul speaks of an anti-Christ to appear at a future time. This prophecy was fulfilled when the pope of Rome appeared and set himself up claiming the authority of God. The pope is that "son of perdition" referred to in Second Thessalonians 2:3, and more distinctly disclosed in the words "whom the Lord shall consume with the spirit of his mouth, and shall destroy with the brightness of his coming" (2 Thess. 2:8b).

God Is Preparing His Army

The Word, the Spirit, and the church stand as God's answer to a world of chaos. The prophecies clearly define all these as God's witnesses being especially active at the close of the age. These are the forces of God to combat the powers of iniquity at our Armageddon. The saints may be as small in number as the few Jewish priests at literal Armageddon, and the host of the enemy may be as numerous as the sand of the sea—but God is with the trinity of righteousness and promises victory. One of the most thrilling scenes of the Revelation comes in the nineteenth chapter when John exclaims:

> And I saw heaven opened, and behold a white horse; and he that sat upon him was called Faithful and True, and in righteousness he doth judge and make war.
>
> His eyes were as a flame of fire, and on his head were many crowns; and he had a name written, that no man knew, but he himself. And he was clothed with a vesture dipped in blood: and his name is called The Word of God.
>
> And the armies which were in heaven followed him upon white horses, clothed in fine linen, white and clean.
>
> And out of his mouth goeth a sharp sword, that with it he should smite the nations: and he shall rule them with a rod of iron: and he treadeth the winepress of the fierceness and wrath of Almighty God.
>
> And he hath on his vesture and on his thigh a name written, KING OF KINGS, AND LORD OF LORDS.
>
> And I saw an angel standing in the sun; and he cried with a loud voice, saying to all the fowls that fly in the midst of heaven, Come and gather yourselves together unto the supper of the great God;
>
> That ye may eat the flesh of kings, and the flesh of captains, and the flesh of mighty men, and the flesh of horses, and of them that sit on them, and the flesh of all men, both free and bond, both small and great.
>
> And I saw the beast, and the kings of the earth, and their armies, gathered together to make war against him that sat on the horse, and against his army.

And the beast was taken, and with him the false prophet that wrought miracles before him, with which he deceived them that had received the mark of the beast, and them that worshiped his image. These both were cast alive into a lake of fire burning with brimstone" (Rev. 19:11-20).

The same white horse, the symbol of pure Christianity, is as holy, pure, and powerful at the end of the age as she was in her primitive existence. One thing must be noted, however. In the beginning the rider of the white horse had only one crown; but at the end of the conflict, many crowns were on his head. These are the crowns of victory won in the battles of earth. The same weapon is brought to the aid of righteousness—a sword out of the mouth of the King of Kings. This is the acclamation that His word cannot be destroyed and remains the chief instrument of warfare against the enemy. It will also be noted that the church of the current century is identically the same as the body of Christ revealed in the New Testament. In Spirit and in the doctrine of the Word, there must be complete agreement in the church. While the church of today, no longer an infant but more mature, uses tools of today's world and has developed many new methods to accomplish her task, her nature must still be identical to the nature of Jesus Christ.

Beyond the dark clouds of the enemies' host the Sun of Righteousness still shines. He has never forgotten His saints and has been working steadily in this conflict against Satan. It is very encouraging to observe the hunger in the hearts of Christians for fellowship together.

Church of God Christians in Germany report that there are still many true saints in Russia. Recently, a Christian walked forty miles just to have fellowship with other saints. A group of Christians sought an underground place of safety to read and disperse the Holy Bible. There were not sufficient copies for all to have complete Bibles, so pages were torn out in sections and distributed among the saints. Only the Spirit creates such a desire for truth, fellowship, and unity. It is heartening to share with numerous Christians the revival of Bible study with renewed vigor. I believe we are on the threshold of one of the greatest moments in church history. It is the responsibility of the church to sound the trumpet of truth and practice the message of Christian unity. It is God's part to draw His sheep into one fold by his Spirit. Unity is a result, not a cause.

In many countries where Christians face persecution, imprisonment, and death, a new bond of love and concern for fellow Christians has been realized. The emphasis is not on straining points of theological differences, but rather in spiritual fellowship as children in God's family. Evangelist Billy Graham states, "the Communists in Russia guard Christianity like Roman soldiers guarded Jesus' tomb; fearful that He would rise again." We firmly believe that true Christianity cannot be buried—it will rise again in Russia!

The prophecies do proclaim a true restoration of the pure gospel message before our Lord's return. Often Christians plead for Christ to answer their prayers; Christ also pleads a prayer that only Christians can answer. It is our Lord's prayer, "that they may be one" (John 17:11).

Jesus prophesied the proclamation of the gospel being complete before His return. He said, "And this gospel of the kingdom shall be preached in all the world for a witness unto all nations; and then shall the end come" (Matt. 24:14). The Revelator, John, bears witness to this truth when he calls attention to the message of three angels who appear in his vision of the Lamb on Mount Zion at the end of time: "And I saw another angel fly in the midst of heaven, having the everlasting gospel to preach to them that dwell on the earth, and to every nation, and kindred, and tongue, and people, Saying with a loud voice, Fear God, and give glory to him; for the hour of his judgment is come; and worship him that made heaven, and earth, and the sea, and the fountains of waters" (Rev. 14:6-7).

It is noted that it is not a new gospel, but rather the everlasting message delivered from the beginning of the gospel day.

A second angel followed proclaiming, "Babylon is fallen, is fallen, that great city, because she made all nations drink of the wine of the wrath of her fornication. And the third angel followed them, saying with a loud voice, If any man worship the beast and his image, and receive his mark in his forehead, or in his hand, the same shall drink the wine of the wrath of God, which is poured out without mixture into the cup of his indignation; and he shall be tormented with fire and brimstone in the presence of the holy angels, and in the presence of the Lamb" (Rev. 14:8-10).

The picture is clear that just preceding God's judgment upon Roman Catholicism and Protestant systems marked with the nature of the apostate church, God would revive the everlasting gospel message with a renewed power of the Holy Spirit. The proclamation of the Word is the only solid foundation for true unity. Mergers of religious denominations and sects which include individuals who deny the virgin birth, Christ's divinity, divine inspiration of the Scriptures, the atonement of Jesus' blood, and the miracles and supernatural religion, certainly have no agreement with the Word. Church councils may form a neutral creed agreeable to numerous religious bodies, but the true church must abide by the only creed God gave for His church—the Bible.

Church councils may succeed in uniting many religious bodies into one union, but men are powerless to breathe the life of the Spirit into its corpse. Spiritual life is not a result of human effort. Only when the Holy Spirit is recognized to be the sole Organizer of the church can life be breathed into the body. Paul said, "For by one Spirit are we all baptized into one body" (1 Cor. 12:13a). To unite Christians who are alive in Christ with the dead bodies of religious creeds is to tie living saints with dead sinners; both suffer separation from God. When a true baptism of the Holy Spirit is experienced by God's children, their natures are changed and they are partakers of the Divine Spirit. Paul said, "If any man have not the Spirit of Christ, he is none of his" (Rom. 8:9b).

The nature of the Word, the Spirit, and the church must be in perfect agreement. This is a prerequisite for Christian unity.

The church has been a sleeping giant which must be awakened with the trumpet sound of war against the powers of evil. Every preacher should shout, "This is Armageddon!" Christian soldiers cannot afford to lay aside their shield of faith, for Satan's darts of atheism, fear, materialism and pagan philosophies will soon reach the target. Helmets of salvation must be tightened lest the enemy find God's soldiers unprepared. Skill in wielding our sword of the Spirit may mean spiritual life or death. A breastplate of righteousness is the only kind of armor that sin cannot penetrate. Only loins girded about with truth are protected from error. Feet shod with the gospel of peace march forward with the weapons of our warfare which "are not carnal, but mighty through God to the pulling down of strong holds" (2 Cor. 10:4).

One of the mightiest victories for Satan is won when Christians are deceived into believing that Armageddon is a literal battle in the future with some anti-Christ who is half man and half devil. Paul said long ago, "For we wrestle not against flesh and blood, but against principalities, against powers, against rulers of the darkness of this world, against **spiritual** wickedness in high places" (Eph. 6:12).

Now, pit the armies of the pagan dragon, the papal beast, and the false prophet against the powers of God, the Word, the Spirit, and the church! The battle is costly and demands trained soldiers. The stakes are high. There will be many casualties; but victory is promised to the saints. God's soldiers may be beheaded but they will say with Paul, "I have fought a good fight, I have finished my course, I have kept the faith: henceforth there is laid up for me a crown of righteousness, which the Lord, the righteous judge, shall give me at that day: and not unto me only, but unto all them also that love his appearing" (2 Tim. 4:7-8). This brings assurance that when the battle is over, "we shall wear a crown in the new Jerusalem."

Christians rejoice to see the gospel reaching around the world. There is a revival spirit awakening, church growth and missions is on the move! In countries where missionaries are not permitted, the radio is reaching. It was a great achievement when Dr. Billy Graham was the speaker for the Global Crusade. On Sunday, April 14, 1996, during prime time, Billy Graham broadcast his Message of Hope to more people around the world than on any day in history.

In his largest and most challenging endeavor yet, Graham reached more than 2.5 billion people in 200 countries—160 on national television and more than 40 via satellite. It was translated into over 40 of the world's most commonly spoken languages and 445 million pieces of follow-up literature was distributed. One million churches in the U.S. and around the world were invited to mobilize "house television gatherings" for this evangelistic effort.

The Trans World Radio reports there has been an increase of 20 million new Chinese Christians in just the past two years.[1]

The thousands of men who joined together for prayer and spiritual commitment is a wonderful experience. These Promise Keepers are making a better home for their families and a better world for others.

Prison Ministry calls for the church to redouble their efforts. Chairman Chuck Colson reports the inmate population at mid year 1997, to be the shocking number of 1,725,842.

We are thankful for the number of missionaries who serve in the United States and countries abroad. We have learned missionaries are never beggars. They are ambassadors who give us the opportunity to become partners by giving our dollars while they give their lives.

The Church of God Movement at Armageddon

In the year 1880, D. S. Warner, along with a number of other saints, caught a vision of a completely restored church.

---

[1]Christian Brotherhood Hour *People to People* publication

The group multiplied, and has been referred to as the Last Reformation, Church of God Reformation, Evening Light, or as Church of God. It is both inclusive and exclusive. The sole requirement for membership is the new birth. God alone could keep such a membership record. The church maintains that any religious body which excludes Christ as the Head is not His Church. Neither is any religious body which excludes some of God's children the body of Christ.

All truth revealed through the great reformers is graciously accepted by the Church of God. The message of Christian unity is especially of great concern. The teachings of Alexander Campbell, founder of the Christian Church, stressed much doctrine regarding this matter. He laid a great emphasis on the Word, producing unity among believers. About the middle of the nineteenth century there was a great holiness movement, termed an Interdenominational Assembly, which stressed the importance of the Holy Spirit experience uniting all Christians. The Church of God ministry proclaims that both the Word and the Spirit are essential to Christian unity. I like what Dr. A. F. Gray has to say:

> The entire Christian world is discussing Christian unity and is experimenting in the pursuit of it. But the assumption seems to be that success in this venture must be achieved at the top level. The heads and leaders of denominations are looked to as ones who must solve the problem of church unity among Christians.
>
> President Eisenhower, in connection with his European trip, said something like this, "The peoples of the world want peace; the governments had better get out of their way." Why should not Christian unity spring from the "grass roots" rather than waiting for church leaders to effect it?[2]

Satan is making a desperate attack on the Church of God message of unity. He presents the temptation to compromise truth in exchange for prestige in religious councils. The enemy pre-

---

[2]Gray, A. F., *The Nature of the Church,* Warner Press, p. 75.

sents a rosy picture of coexistence with all religious bodies rather than proclaiming the unique pattern for the church. The leaders of spiritual Babylon are calling loud and long for the return of the saints to the fleshpots of materialism. Satan even suggests that the Church of God has fulfilled her mission, made her contribution, and should now lose her identity like the gulf stream that flows into an ocean. Nothing could be further from the truth!

True saints who have been delivered from the confusion and bondage of Babylon have no desire to return. The Protestant body is no more spiritual now than when they left it. Wise Christians will not accept the counterfeit of union for genuine unity.

Saints who stand on Mount Zion have only the Father's name in their foreheads and follow the Lamb wherever He leads.

Harold Boyer previously served as chairman of the General Ministerial Assembly of the Church of God, writes the following in his book, *The Apostolic Church.* "There is a distinctiveness to this reformation movement of the Church of God. It does not seek to reform either the Roman Catholic, state, or Protestant church; it rather seeks to call the true people of God from all humanly organized churches to true spiritual unity, thus establishing on earth the church of the New Testament. Your writer believes the truth to be restored. I believe we have the truth, but greatly fear the truth does not have us. Too many professed saints are indifferent, and not a few have backed away to become engulfed again in the spirit of Babylon confusion, but the truth goes marching on."[3]

The Church of God is unique. Because of its nature it cannot merge or unite with systems contrary to Christ. The body of Christ is holy and cannot be joined to councils, synods or assemblies which include in their membership unregenerated persons. Neither can the church adhere to ecclesiastical governments of human origin, for the church is divinely governed. The only pattern for unity is the New Testament pattern. Anything

---

[3]Boyer, Harold, *The Apostolic Church,* Warner Press, Anderson, Indiana p. 58.

else is not the design of God. True unity cannot be realized on the terms of men; the Lord Himself has set the price.

May God grant that the Church of God movement shall stand in the front ranks of the greatest spiritual conflict of the ages.

There is an urgent call to awaken the church. All too long the church has been weak, tardy, irrelevant and silent. Weak saints become strong, healthy hypocrites. Let's all check our armor. Jesus, our Captain, is calling for all soldiers to be better prepared for battle; learn how to use our sword of the Spirit.

The Army of the Lord

In the holy army we've enlisted,
Now the banner of the cross we bear;
All the forces of the wrong resisted,
Causes right to triumph everywhere.
We will follow where our Captain leadeth,
We will fight against the sullen foe.
We will stand together, then we'll conquer;
Certain victory is ours, we know.

We will push the fight o'er land and ocean,
And across the desert plains of sin;
We will give the cause our true devotion,
Till for truth and righteousness we win,
We're arrayed in all the gospel armor,
Bravely onward we will ever go,
Till we put to flight the hosts of evil,
Through our Leader we'll subdue the foe.

Hear the tramping of the countless millions,
Hear the battle's mighty thunders roar;
Hear the great Commander of the army
Sound the orders loud from shore to shore;
"Go ye into all the world, I'm with you,
Take the fortresses of sin today,
Charge the enemy, compel surrender,
Wear the victor's crown through endless day.

B. E. Warren [4]

---

[4]Warren, B. E., "The Army of the Lord," *Church of God Hymnal*, p. 226, copyright 1953, The Gospel Trumpet Company.

The Second Resurrection

"For the Lord himself shall descend from heaven with a shout, with the voice of the archangel, and with the trump of God: and the dead in Christ shall rise first: Then we which are alive and remain shall be caught up together with them in the clouds, to meet the Lord in the air: and so shall we ever be with the Lord" (1 Thess. 4:16-17).

Here, Paul describes the manner of our Lord's return. He explains to the Thessalonian Christians that the saints who are alive at Christ's coming will not be taken to heaven until all those saints who have died have been resurrected.

In Jesus' sermon concerning the two resurrections, it is clear also that all those in the graves, good or bad, will come forth. "Marvel not at this: for the hour is coming, in the which all they that are in the graves shall hear his voice and shall come forth; they that have done good, unto the resurrection of life; and they that have done evil, unto the resurrection of damnation" (John 5:28-29). Paul further proclaims, "So also is the resurrection of the dead. It [the body] is sown in corruption; it is raised in incorruption: It is sown a natural body; it is raised a spiritual body" (1 Cor. 15:42, 44a).

What a day that will be! The earth will tremble and shake. It will burst asunder at the voice of God and yield up all the dead from the ages of time. John describes, "And the sea gave up the dead which were in it; and death and hell delivered up the dead which were in them: and they were judged every man according to their works" (Rev. 20:13).

The second resurrection is of the physical body. The great Creator who remembers to awaken the pulseless heart of an acorn in the sod will not forget even one of the human creatures created in His own image. The resurrection of Jesus Christ is the great witness to the immortality of man. Ever since the day Christ used the cross for a battering ram to burst the gates of death asunder, Christians firmly believe the acclamation of the Victor over death saying, "Because I live, ye shall live also" (John 14:19b).

There is little need to question the nature of the resurrected body. John simply states, "Beloved, now are we the sons of God, and it doth not yet appear what we shall be: but we know that, when he shall appear, we shall be like him: for we shall see him as he is" (1 John 3:2). Glory to the Lord—He wore a robe of flesh like mine, that I might wear a glorified body like His!

When the Lord returns He will not again take upon Himself the clothing of the flesh and reign upon the earth. Rather He will clothe the saints with immortality and take them to reign with Him. It is truly written, "Flesh and blood cannot inherit the kingdom of God; neither doth corruption inherit incorruption" (1 Cor. 15:50).

Some have supposed there were two literal resurrections— one for the righteous, and a resurrection of the wicked later. It is maintained that the righteous dead and alive will all be caught secretly away with Christ, leaving the wicked people on earth for a great tribulation. Jesus preached concerning this matter; four times in one sermon He declared that the righteous would be resurrected on the **last** day. "And this is the Father's will which hath sent me, that of all which he hath given me I should lose nothing, but should raise it up again at the last day. And this is the will of him that sent me, that everyone which seeth the Son, and believeth on him, may have everlasting life; and I will raise him up at the last day" (John 6:39-40). (See verses 44-54 also.)

The same truth is expounded in the parables. In the Parable of the Tares, it is noted that the tares are **first** gathered, then the wheat is placed into the garner; but both grow together until the end. Jesus' description of the judgment reveals both sheep and goats before Him at the same time; likewise the fish are separated, the good from the bad, in the Parable of the Net and Fishes.

There are many appointments we may break; but no one will fail to rise for an appointment with God at the resurrection day. We will **all** be there together.

The Destruction of the Earth

Recent scientific research and nuclear weapons for warfare have created much concern regarding the destruction of the planet named earth. Many scientists once believed the world was indestructible. Now, however, scientists realize they have at their command hydrogen and cobalt bombs capable of utter holocaust destroying all life on this planet. Mononuclear weapons have been discovered which are too deadly to even use in test bombing.

God always vindicates His Word. Jesus very plainly referred to the end of the world saying, "lo, I am with you alway, even unto the end of the world" (Matt. 28:20b). Again He proclaimed, "Heaven and earth shall pass away, but my words shall not pass away" (Matt. 24:35).

Peter makes a vivid description of the earth being consumed:

> "But the day of the Lord will come as a thief in the night; in the which the heavens shall pass away with a great noise, and the elements shall melt with fervent heat, the earth also and the works that are therein shall be burned up. Seeing then that all these things shall be dissolved, what manner of persons ought ye to be in all holy conversation and godliness, Looking for and hasting unto the coming of the day of God, wherein the heavens being on fire shall be dissolved, and the elements shall melt with fervent heat? Nevertheless we, according to his promise, look for new heavens and a new earth, wherein dwelleth righteousness" (II Pet. 3:10-13).

John describes the catalysis as a mighty earthquake, the sun becoming as sackcloth of hair and the moon turning to blood. In his vision he beheld the stars falling from the heavens as figs being shaken from a fig tree by a mighty wind. The heavens departed as a scroll and every mountain and island was moved out of its place (See Rev. 6:12-17).

It is readily observed from the Scriptures that Christ is not coming to renovate this planet. Rather, He will come to consummate this time world of materialism. The planetary heavens will vanish as a vapor. The earthly elements which have been the habitation of evil as well as good will be annihilated. The ground which was cursed because of Adam's sin (Gen. 3:17-19) shall cease to be and the dust from which man was created and unto which he returned will disappear in a great blast. Thus shall it be fulfilled as the Psalmist has written, "Of old thou hast laid the foundation of the earth; and the heavens are the work of thy hands. They shall perish, but thou shalt endure" (Ps. 102:25-26a). And the words of the prophet shall come to pass as he said, "The earth is utterly broken down, the earth is clean dissolved, the earth is moved exceedingly. The earth shall reel to and fro like a drunkard, and shall be removed like a cottage; . . . it shall fall, and not rise again" (Isa. 24:19-20). When this great day appears I want to be safe in the bosom of God!

The Judgment Day

One of the most solemn thoughts a man is capable of thinking is of the truth of the judgment day. The Scriptures declare that God "hath appointed a day, in which he will judge the world in righteousness by that man whom he hath ordained" (Acts 17:31). "That man" refers to Christ.

From Paul we learn that the judgment day will be the day of Christ's coming. He wrote to Timothy explaining about "the Lord Jesus Christ, who shall judge the quick and the dead **at his appearing** and his kingdom" (2 Tim. 4:1). In Daniel's apocalyptic book he draws the picture of the judgment vividly: "I beheld till the thrones were cast down, and the Ancient of days did sit, whose garment was white as snow, and the hair of his head like pure wool: his throne was like the fiery flame, and his wheels as burning fire. A fiery stream issued and came forth from before Him; thousand thousands ministered unto him, and ten thousand times ten thousand stood before him; the judgment was set, and the books were opened" (Dan. 7:9-10).

Christ portrays the same scene uttering, "When the Son of man shall come in his glory, and all the holy angels with him, then shall he sit upon the throne of his glory; and before him shall be gathered all nations; and he shall separate them one from another, as a shepherd divideth his sheep from the goats" (Matt. 25:31-32).

The Revelation describes it with the metaphor of a harvest and also the gathering of grapes (Rev. 14:14-20). Each figure of speech expresses that the judgment will take place immediately following the coming of the Lord.

The absolute justice of God demands a judgment day. If there is no judgment, then God is not just. Often in this world men become victims of the erring, fallible judgment of human minds. Frequently true justice is not meted out in this present world; the righteous are oppressed and the wicked exalted. It would often appear that men who do evil would escape punishment. While it is a fact that some people do a great deal of reaping in this world, it is also evident that a judgment is necessary in order to fulfill justice.

The only sins which will not appear at the judgment are those that have been blotted out, washed away and buried in the sea of forgetfulness by Jesus' blood.

An elderly Christian doctor sat with a dying patient who expressed fear of meeting God. In an effort to quiet the fears of his friend, the doctor explained, "If your sins are gone you need not fear God any more than a child would fear going to a loving father."

The doctor continued the thought as he told about his faithful dog, Rover. "Rover followed me closely all the way through the storm as I walked the long distance to your home. Now he is waiting outside your bedroom door. He has never been inside this room before. The room is quite dark and the dog would have no way of knowing what was in this place. But I would only need to open the door and call his name and he would leap into this room. He is eager to come, even into the unknown place, because he knows his master is here. You see, my friend, if your sins are forgiven and you have followed Christ closely, you need not fear when He opens the door of death and calls your name. You know the Master is in the unknown room beyond."

Paul speaks of those whose sins have already passed judgment: "Some men's sins are open beforehand, going before to judgment; and some men they follow after" (1 Tim. 5:24). Every soul may be sure that if he dies in his sins, his sins will follow him to the throne of judgment. Paul says, "For we must all appear before the judgment seat of Christ: that every one may receive the things done in his body, according to that he hath done, whether it be good or bad. Knowing therefore the terror of the Lord, we persuade men" (2 Cor. 5 :10-11).

I am persuaded that hidden in the mind of man there is a record of his deeds, thoughts, attitudes, and motives. There have been people who bear testimony to the fact that in a moment of crucial danger a vivid flash of memory startled them. In a split second their whole lives blazed before the conscious mind and they knew the judgment God placed upon them in that moment. Will not the great day of God's judgment come in a similar manner? The individual's book of memory which gives the account of his life written by his own deeds will open in the presence of Christ, the Judge, who holds in His hand the Word of God and the Book of Life.

This final judgment will pass sentence on all intelligent creatures. Peter tells of fallen angels who have been reserved in darkness awaiting this day of justice: "For if God spared not the angels that sinned, but cast them down to hell, and delivered them into chains of darkness, to be reserved unto judgment . . ." (2 Pet. 2:4). Jude refers to the same matter saying, "And the angels which kept not their first estate, but left their own habitation, he hath reserved in everlasting chains under darkness unto the judgment of the great day" (Jude 1:6).

Recall the words the demons asked Christ when they were cast out of the man who said his name was Legion: "What have we to do with thee, Jesus, thou Son of God? art thou come hither to torment us before the time?" (Matt. 8:29). The judgment will be that time of final doom.

On the day of judgment, Satan, prince of devils, shall be cast into hell and all the evil powers of iniquity with him. His deceived victims who have walked in darkness and become slaves must spend eternity in a hell prepared for the devil and his angels. What an assemblage will appear at the judgment—saints, sinners, angels and devils!

Rewards Will Be Received

Hear the Christ saying, "Behold, I come quickly; and my reward is with me, to give every man according as his work shall be. He that is unjust, let him be unjust still: and he which is filthy, let him be filthy still: and he that is righteous, let him be righteous still: and he that is holy, let him be holy still" (Rev. 22:12, 11). There will be no time to change your way of living after Christ comes. Yea, the destiny of every soul is sealed at the moment of physical death.

A misunderstanding is sometimes created when reference is given concerning rewards of the deceased. It is commonly expressed, "They have passed to their reward." Truly, Jesus said to the dying thief, "Today shalt thou be with me in paradise" (Luke 23 :43b). Stephen expressed seeing Christ standing to receive him into this place of bliss. Our Lord called attention to Lazarus being carried to Abraham's bosom. (This refers to the bosom of the Father as Abraham was the father of the Jews.) Paul also expressed, "We are confident, I say, and willing rather to be absent from the body, and to be present with the Lord" (2 Cor. 5:8). However, final rewards of the mansion, the crown, and the glories of heaven are not experienced immediately at death. By the same token the wicked are in a place of torment, like a condemned prisoner in the death cell, knowing his sentence, and awaiting execution; but final punishment will be meted out after the judgment.

When one dies there are three things that happen: (1) The soul must meet God and await final judgment in paradise or torment; (2) The body returns to the earth from whence it came;

(3) The influence of the deceased, good or bad, continues in this present world. There is no casket large enough to hold a man's influence. Rewards are not received until the end of time when all influence is terminated.

For example, note a devoted Christian mother whose children are all unsaved. In her lifetime she earnestly prays, teaches, and sets a godly example. She passes away before her prayers are answered. The influence of the mother's prayers continue long after she is deceased. Each one of the children becomes a Christian. How grateful this mother will be in eternity that her influence lived on. In one's life-span one sets influences in motion which are like making investments in stock. Only eternity can reveal the dividends.

Jesus promised, "The Son of man shall come in the glory of his Father with his angels; and **then** he shall reward every man according to his works" (Matt. 16:27). Paul understood this truth when he wrote "Henceforth there is laid up for me a crown of righteousness, which the Lord, the righteous judge, shall give me at that day" (2 Tim. 4:8a).

Reward of the Wicked

Recent polls taken in universities as well as in theological schools reveal that a large percentage of persons do not believe in future punishment. Both within the religious realm and the secular world one may find a large company of unbelievers. But to join their ranks is to part company with Christ. Jesus believes in future punishment. He preached more sermons warning against going to hell than He preached about heaven. Christ is the Preacher who draws the judgment scene so vividly and explains the destiny of those on His left hand. "Then shall he say also unto them on the left hand, Depart from me, ye cursed, into everlasting fire, prepared for the devil and his angels. And these shall go away into everlasting punishment" (Matt. 25:41, 46a).

We love the beautiful parables of the Lord recorded in the fifteenth chapter of Luke. Here He gives three examples of seeking the lost: the lost sheep, the lost coin, and the lost son. Christ impresses us with the love of God in going to great measure to restore the lost. The sixteenth chapter of Luke tells the story of Dives and Lazarus. It is important to remember that the same preacher tells all these stories.

It is well to observe from the story of Dives and Lazarus that the rich man was in torment for what he had failed to do rather than from sins of commission. It cannot be overlooked that our Lord said there was a great gulf fixed between paradise and torment and no one could pass over that gulf. This is evidence that hell is not a place of purging where one gradually climbs a ladder and reaches release by mass being said or prayers being prayed. The selfish nature of Dives remained unchanged after death. Even in torment he could not think of others. He asked for water to cool his tongue but gave no consideration to the burning tongues of those around him. It was for his brothers that he requested Lazarus to return to earth with salvation's message. No thought is expressed for the relatives of others in the regions of the lost.

Jesus warned, "And fear not them which kill the body, but are not able to kill the soul: but rather fear him which is able to destroy both soul and body in hell" (Matt. 10:28). Paul conveys the same thought in writing to the Thessalonians. "When the Lord shall be revealed from heaven with his mighty angels, in flaming fire taking vengeance on them that know not God, and that obey not the gospel of our Lord Jesus Christ: Who shall be punished with everlasting destruction from the presence of the Lord" (2 Thess. 1:7b-9a).

The Revelation gives much consideration to the judgments of God and the final doom of the wicked. Nearing the conclusion of the great Revelation John exclaims, "But the fearful, and unbelieving, and the abominable, and murderers, and whoremongers, and sorcerers, and idolaters, and all liars, shall have their part in the lake which burneth with fire and brimstone: which is the second death" (Rev. 21:8).

Reward of the Righteous

We Have a Hope

Have we any hope within us of a life beyond the grave
In the fair and vernal lands?
Do we know that when our earthly house by death shall be dissolved
We've a house not made with hands?

Blessed hope we have within us is an anchor to the soul,
It is both steadfast and sure;
It is founded on the promises of Father's written word,
And 'twill evermore endure.

Since we've walked the strait and narrow way our path has ever shone
Brighter, brighter, day by day;
Hope within our hearts assures us it is better farther on,
It is brighter all the way.

Life will end in joyful singing, "I have fought a faithful fight,"
Then we'll lay our armor down;
And our spirits freed from earthly ties shall take their happy flight,
To possess a starry crown.

Chorus:
We have a hope within our souls,
Brighter than the perfect day
God has given us His Spirit,
And we want the world to hear it
All our doubts are passed away.

W. G. Schell [5]

To stand at Christ's right hand and hear Him say, "Come ye blessed of my Father, inherit the kingdom prepared for you from the foundation of the world" (Matt. 25:34b), will repay a million times every trial, cross, persecution or heartache we have endured on the narrow road. The saints shall join with Peter in sharing the inheritance he saw by faith as he wrote, "To an inheritance incorruptible, and undefiled, and that fadeth not away, reserved in heaven for you" (1 Pet. 1:4). This will be the crown-

---

[5]Schell, W. G., "We Have A Hope," *Hymnal of the Church of God*, p, 443, copyright 1971, Warner Press, Inc.

ing day when the saints are all made heirs of the kingdom with Christ.

What a glorious moment when the Scriptures are fulfilled which say, "Then cometh the end, when he shall have delivered up the kingdom of God, even the Father" (1 Cor. 15:24a). And the saints shall hear the seventh angel shout and join a tumult of voices saying, "The kingdoms of this world are become the kingdoms of our Lord, and of his Christ; and he shall reign for ever and ever" (Rev. 11:15b).

It will be a great Palm Sunday when the gates of the new Jerusalem which is above swing wide and the King of Glory enters in with all the hosts of the redeemed in the procession, waving palms of victory and clad in white robes ready for the marriage supper of the Lamb. What joy to cast our crowns before him and cry aloud, "Worthy is the Lamb that was slain to receive power, and riches, and wisdom, and strength, and honour and glory, and blessing" (Rev. 5:12b).

The New Heaven and the New Earth

As pilgrims and sojourners in this world below, the righteous of every generation have sought an eternal city whose Builder and Maker is God. Jesus promised to go and prepare such a place. "I go to prepare a place for you. And if I go and prepare a place for you, I will come again, and receive you unto myself; that where I am, there ye may be also" (John 14:2b-3).

It is this holy city, the place Jesus went to prepare, that John describes as his vision climaxing the Revelation, saying, "And I saw a new heaven and a new earth: for the first heaven and the first earth were passed away" (Rev. 21:la). John comprehended in a vision what Peter saw by faith when he foretold the destruction of the earth, then hastened to say, "Nevertheless we, according to his promise, look for new heavens and a new earth, wherein dwelleth righteousness" (2 Pet. 3:13).

With the passing of the earthly sphere of planetary heavens and this earth, a new world becomes the habitation of the saints.

In the heavens of that eternal dwelling place there is "no need of the sun, neither of the moon, to shine in it: for the glory of God did lighten it, and the Lamb is the light thereof" (Rev. 21:23). Storm clouds or dark curtains of night will be unknown because "there shall be no night there" (Rev. 21:25b). The new earth shall be free from the curse of sin; thorns and thistles shall not encumber the fields of glory. The tree of life abundantly yields fruit perpetually for the healing of the nations. These beautiful symbols indicate a realm of perfection where sin's curse is forbidden.

The language of contrasts throughout the Revelation reaches a grand climax as the author draws a striking comparison between the Garden of Eden and the garden of glory. At Eden the tempter entered in to destroy holiness. But John exclaims that in the heavenly garden, "There shall in no wise enter into it any thing that defileth, neither whatsoever worketh abomination, or maketh a lie; but they which are written in the Lamb's book of life" (Rev. 21:27). There was a forbidden tree in Eden but the heavenly abode, the tree of life, is for everyone.

Genesis tells of a river in the midst of the garden. John also saw in heaven "a pure river of water of life, clear as crystal, proceeding out of the throne of God and of the Lamb" (Rev. 22:1). How beautifully the truth is conveyed that only out of the heart of God can life flow. Like a fountain of living water, Christ has satisfied the souls of His saints who have been partakers of the living water to never thirst again. Will not the woman of Samaria tell again of her joy in receiving this living water?

Trudging from Eden's paradise, Adam and Eve experienced the first drops of moisture flowing from their eyes. Tears—what are they? Ever since that day, tears have fallen from the eyes of all the earthly family; but in heaven "God shall wipe away all tears from their eyes; and there shall be no more death, neither sorrow, nor crying, neither shall there be any more pain: for the former things are passed away" (Rev. 21:4).

No more death! Death has reigned since the day Cain slew Abel; but the grim monster shall never enter the gates of the holy city. What joy, rapture, and bliss to clasp in our arms again our loved ones who have been severed from earthly ties by the power of death's sword. And shall we know them? Indeed, if by divine revelation the disciples knew Moses and Elijah, whom they had never seen on earth, but recognized them at the Transfiguration, shall we not know those whom we have loved? If Lazarus and Dives, separated by a great gulf, could identify each other beyond the grave, shall we not know those who stand at our side? If the disciples knew the Christ in His resurrected body, is it not a token of promise that we too shall know even as we are known? How glorious the thought that separation shall never come again! Blessed happiness shall abide where life reigns forever and death is completely slain. The little child we committed to the Lord long ago at the graveside shall tell of loving care the angel nursemaids gave. Their little cheeks once pale with death will glow with vibrant pink. The lines of age on Mother's face have been erased and Father's step is no longer cautious and slow. Love for departed companions is born anew with a deeper and richer experience. There are no cries of suffering heard and no one writhes in pain; there is no sorrow in our Father's house. No bodies are crippled, diseased, or maimed in that eternal land.

It is recorded that Adam and Eve were forced out of the garden and banished from communion with God; but John tells that the redeemed shall always abide around His throne. He writes, "And they shall see his face; and his name shall be in their foreheads" (Rev. 22:4).

It is significant that Ezekiel also had a vision of the heavenly city (Ezek. 40) many years prior to John's Revelation. Much of the description given by John is similar to the vision of the ancient prophet. The measurements, the jasper walls, the precious stones, and gates of pearl are beyond the comprehension of mortal minds. It must be remembered that John has used symbols and figurative language to accommodate the finite mind. Heaven's glories cannot be described with words of mortal tongues. Paul found the grandeur of paradise unspeakable and experienced such ecstasy he found it unlawful to utter words of description.

A little boy who had been born blind received sight following skilled surgery. The first sight before his eyes was his mother's face. "How beautiful, how beautiful!" the lad exclaimed. When first he saw the beauties of nature he cried, "Mother, Mother, why didn't you tell me it was so beautiful?" Gently the mother replied, "I tried, my child, but I couldn't make you understand." So shall it be with God's children. When scales of mortality drop from the eyes of the soul we too shall exclaim, "My Lord, my Lord, how beautiful You are!" When heaven is unfolded we shall cry aloud, "Why didn't You tell me how beautiful it was?" The Christ shall say, "I tried, My child, but you couldn't comprehend!"

Nothing is left to be desired in our Father's house. It is noted that John sees all needs, as we understand them in the physical, being supplied. For shelter, there is a mansion; for clothing, there is a robe; for food, there is the fruit of the tree of life; for water, there is a river; for light, there is the Sun of Righteousness. Heaven is the land of complete fulfillment.

It is very obvious that John uses negatives, or what is not in heaven, to describe its glory. This is because we have experienced the result of sins and can in a measure comprehend how wonderful a world would be without them. However, there are also some positive things made known about this holy place.

It is a world of **praise.** Even little children shall sing the glad hosannas and saints of every nation shall say, "Blessing, and glory, and wisdom, and thanksgiving, and honor, and power, and might, be unto our God for ever and ever. Amen" (Rev. 7:12). Music shall echo and reecho again and again through heaven's courts.

It is a world of **prayer**. Even Jesus did not cease praying after the resurrection. He is now in the presence of the Father praying. We, too, shall pray in the holy city—face to face with God.

It is a world of **service.** It is true that we enter into rest, but this is rest from the labors of earth. In the realms above, the saints do not sit around twiddling their thumbs. John says, "and his servants shall serve him" (Rev. 22:3b).

I am persuaded that it is a great world of **knowledge.** When I get there I want to have Paul teach me about theology, and I want John and Daniel to be instructors in eschatology. Heaven holds millions of secrets our souls shall thrill to gleam. Greatest of all, it is a positive truth that the great Teacher, Saviour, and Lord, Jesus Christ, will eternally abide in the midst of His saints in a world without end!

How long is eternity? There is an ancient proverb which opens a tiny window of comprehension. The proverb describes all the stone, rock, and granite of the entire earth being heaped into one colossal mountain. It is said that God could send from heaven a tiny sparrow once each hundred years to sharpen its beak upon these rocks. When all the mountain was worn away from visits of the tiny bird, eternity would have only begun!

Future Forecast

The Battle of Armageddon will continue until Jesus comes again. Nations reap what they sow in this time world. America has sown some wicked seeds. We are now reaping the harvest of the seeds of slavery and the reaping is far from ending. Removing God and His commandments from the political arena, the school room, the social world, the work place and the homes of America will continue to force reaping for years to come. Crime, divorce, humanism, gambling, drug addiction and all kinds of sin must have consequences. We sow to the wind and reap a whirl wind. Our children also must bear the sins of parents. Science, technology, government, politics, employment, the economy and all other earthly things have changed. The church must make changes too. People are not as concerned about the church doctrine as they are about their personal and family needs.

It is impossible to change the past. However, just as the current Church of God Reformation Movement is largely the product of the die cast by our predecessors, this generation will form the castings to mold the movement for tomorrow. The difficulty with pioneers is that all too soon they become settlers. We are also tempted to look back in our history for a "golden peak" and endeavor to revert back to a past experience, or at least try to duplicate it. Efforts to return to a past decade are as futile as energies expended by an adult struggling to become an infant. Continued change, growth, and development is the evidence we are a movement—not a denomination. Even if it were possible to reproduce the church of the first century it would obviously be immature and inadequate to serve today's world. To strive for the New Testament pattern in doctrine, evangelism, and fellowship is essential; but a worldwide reproduction of the congregations at Corinth would be a catastrophe.

There are disturbing voices in the religious world today making appalling predictions. Some say, "the church is totally irrelevant" and suggest a churchless Christianity. Others declare "the institutional church is as archaic as a museum collection of fossils, and predict its demise. Critics who would write the obituary of the church speak of the late twentieth century as the "post-Christian age," asserting Biblical concepts are neither intellectually acceptable or culturally valid.

We would tend to simply ignore prophets of doom. However, we are faced with some shocking facts and statistics. The population explosion is primarily in the non-free world. Today five children are born in the non-Christian world for every one child born in the land of liberty.

The world has never been more in need of the true message concerning the church. The immediate future can become the most exciting period in the history of Christianity. God is searching for a body of people who will be fashioned by the Holy Spirit to reveal His design for the church in this age. Exhibiting God's ideal will demand more than slight modifications of procedures for organization, or rearrangement of worship patterns. Innovations, bizarre architecture, and modern techniques are obviously superficial. The change must be more profound.

There is an intrinsic need for a rebirth of Holy Spirit leadership. A bold reaffirmation of the unique message of our movement proclaiming the church is a distinct visible body of believers, free from Satan's bondage, deception, carnality and sectarianism, would produce revival. A strong proclamation of the Word will project clear direction. The Spirit and the Word are God's Agents for continued Reformation.

Castings for the church of the future demand new strategies. The church must be more than a crowd watching a performance. Worship must result in witness. Communion must lead to commitment. Motivation is required to involve all available human resources. Youth must be challenged to worthy goals and excited with hope for tomorrow. Pastors are urged to train and equip the laity to excel in church leadership.

Women have an abundance of untapped energy and skill to contribute toward new ministries. Retired persons need to be inspired to render time and service for extending the kingdom.

This is the day of opportunity for the Reformation Movement. One hundred years of experience establishes confidence. The message of "a united church for a divided world" is most pertinent. Our human resources, material assets, academic skills and techniques are abundant. Communication facilities are fabulous. The refueling of the Holy Spirit is available. The Bible charts our purpose and direction. The "unfinished" Reformation Movement open a new chapter with a future as bright as the promises of God.

Science, technology, government, politics, employment, the economy, and all other earthly things have changed. The church must make changes too. People must be challenged and encouraged to become as concerned about the church doctrine as they are about their personal lives.

The Conclusion

The Apocalypse deals with weighty subjects. Here we see the birth, battles, and victories of the church. It gives great consideration to the kingdoms of men in contrast to the kingdom of God. The truth reveals light concerning the soul, sin, atonement, judgment, and destiny. Christ is depicted as the mighty Conqueror over sin, death and Satan. Eternity's veil is pulled aside and the glimpse of heaven and hell is unfolded. No truth could be of greater concern to the souls of the twentieth century. Of all these truths, **the symbols speak!**

References

Chapter I

[1]Barclay, William, *Letters to the Seven Churches,* New York: Abington Press, 1957, p. 14.

[2]Barclay, William, *Letters to the Seven Churches.*

[3]Smith, F. G., *Revelation Explained*, p. 53, Anderson, Indiana, Warner Press, 1943

[4]Clarke, Adam, *Commentary*, Vol. VI, p. 989, New York, Abingdon-Cokesbury Press

[5]*Clayton Choir Melodies,* #1, Indiana: The Rodeheaver Hall-Mack Company, p. 57. Used by permission.

Chapter II

[1]Evans, Louis H., *This Is America's Hour,* Fleming H. Revell Co., Westwood, N.J., 1957, p. 38.

Chapter III

[1]Smith, F. G., *Revelation Explained,* p. 164., Warner Press, 1943, Anderson, Indiana.

[2]See Time Table, p. 58.

[3]*Grolier Encyclopedia,* Vol. 8, p. 206, New York, 1946.

[4]*Fox's Book of Martyrs*, p. 47. Edited by Forbush, Wm. Zondervan Publishing House, 1926, Grand Rapids, Michigan

[5]See Time Table, p. 58.

[6]Clarke, Adam, *Commentary*, p. 1026, New York, Abingdon-Cokesbury Press.

Chapter IV

[1]See Time Table, p. 58.

Chapter V

[1]*Smith's Bible Dictionary*

[2]Van Baalen, J. K., *Gist of the Cults,* p. 36, William Erdman Publishing Co., 1955, Grand Rapids, Michigan

Chapter VI

[1]*The Voice of the Martyrs*—P.O. Box 443, Bartlesville, OK (used by permission)

[2]Lillie McCutcheon, *Vital Christianity,* May 27. 1979, Anderson, Indiana

[3]*Native Missionary Publication,* Box 277, Joplin, Mo., places the figure at 20-30 million,

[4]*Pulpit Digest,* November, 1955, p. 61, Great Neck, New York

Chapter VII

[1]Brown, C. E., *Reign of Christ,* Warner Press, 1947, Anderson, Indiana, p. 179.

[2]Hillis, Don, *Thirty Pieces of Silver,* Orient Crusades, Los Angeles, Calif.

[3]*Humanist Manifestos I and II,* Prometheus Books, Buffalo, N.Y.

[4]The Columbus, Ohio, *Dispatch* (Newspaper), Friday, March 27, 1998

Chapter VIII

[1]Christian Brotherhood Hour *People to People* publication, Anderson, Indiana

[2]Gray, A. F., *The Nature of the Church,* Warner Press, p. 75. Anderson, Indiana 1960.

[3]Boyer, Harold, *The Apostolic Church,* Warner Press, Anderson, Ind., p. 58.

[4]Warren, B. E., "The Army of the Lord," *Hymnal of the Church of God*, p. 226, The Gospel Trumpet Co., Anderson, Indiana, 1953.

[5]Schell, W. G., "We Have a Hope," *Hymnal of the Church of God,* p. 443, Warner Press, Inc., Anderson, Indiana, 1971.

Acknowledgments

Bales, James D., *Communism—Its Faith and Fallacies,* Grand Rapids, Baker Book House, 1962.

Barclay, William, *Letters to the Seven Churches,* New York-Nashville, Abingdon Press, 1957.

Bennett, John C., *Christianity and Communism,* New York, Haddam House, Association Press, 1949.

Blanshard, Paul, *The Future of Catholic Power,* POAU, Washington, D.C., 1961.

Boettner, Loraine, *Roman Catholicism,* Philadelphia, Presbyterian and Reformed Publishing Company, 1962.

Boyer, Harold W., *The Apostolic Church and the Apostasy,* Anderson, Indiana, Warner Press, 1960.

Brown, Charles E., *The Apostolic Church,* Anderson, Indiana, Warner Press, 1947.

—-*The Reign of Christ,* Anderson, Indiana, Warner Press, 1948.

Dallmann, William, *How Peter Became Pope,* Saint Louis, Missouri, Concordia Publishing House, 1931.

Evans, Louis H., *This Is America's Hour,* Westwood, New Jersey, Fleming H. Revell Company, *1957.*

—-*The Kingdom Is Yours,* Westwood, New Jersey, Fleming H. Revell Company, *1952.*

Forbush, Wm. (Edited by), *Fox's Book of Martyrs,* Grand Rapids, Zondervan Publishing House, 1926.

Fuller, D. O. (Edited by), *Valiant for the Truth,* New York, McGraw-Hill Book Company, Inc., 1961.

Gaulke, Max R., *May Thy Kingdom Come Now,* Anderson, Indiana, Warner Press, 1959.

Gray, Albert F., *The Nature of the Church,* Anderson, Indiana, Warner Press, 1960.

Hillis, Don, *If America Elects a Catholic President,* Findlay, Ohio, Dunham Publishing Co., 1959.

—-*Thirty Pieces of Silver,* Findlay, Ohio, Dunham Publishing Co., 1960. Kempin, Albert I., *Daniel for Today,* Anderson, Indiana, Warner Press, 1952.

Kik, I. Marcellus, *Revelation Twenty,* Philadelphia, Presbyterian and Reformed Publishing Company, *1955.*

Ramsay, William M., *The Letters to the Seven Churches,* Grand Rapids, Baker Book House, 1963.

Riggle, H. M., *Jesus Is Coming Again,* Anderson, Indiana, Warner Press, 1943.

Schwarz, Fred, *The Christian Answer to Communism,* Anderson, Indiana, Great Commission Schools.

—-*You Can Trust the Communists (To Be Communists),* Engelwood Cliffs, New Jersey, Prentice-Hall, Inc., 1960.

Smith, F. G., *Revelation Explained,* Anderson, Indiana, Warner Press, 1943.

Van Baalen, J. K., *The Gist 0/the Cults,* Grand Rapids, William Erdman
Publishing Co., 1955.

Other Resource Material

Adam Clarke Commentary, New York, Abingdon-Cokesbury Press.
Grolier Encyclopedia, New York, 1946.
Smith's Bible Dictionary.

Magazines and Pamphlets

American Sunday School Union, 1816 Chestnut St., Philadelphia 3, Pennsylvania.

Christian Heritage, Sea Cliff, New York.

Church and State, Washington, D.C.

Communist Horror, Pilgrim Tract Society, Randleman, North Carolina.

Exposé: Catholic Plan to Control the U.S., Harry Hampel, P.O. Box 8646, Dallas, Texas.

Native Missionary, Box 277, Joplin, Mo.

Pulpit Digest, Great Neck, New York.

Redbook, Dayton 1, Ohio.

The Convert, Clairton, Pennsylvaniá.

Dateline. National Association of Manufacturers, 2 East 48th St., New York 17, New York.